ROAD MAP
TO YOUR VACATION
PROPERTY DREAM

by Christopher S. Cain

Library of Congress Catalog Card No.: 98-092667

All inquiries should be addressed to:
Christopher Communications, Inc.
1007 Green Branch Court
Oviedo, FL 32765

ISBN 0-914895-01-X

Acknowledgements

The author gratefully acknowledges the following professional participation that helped to bring this book to its present form:

Executive Director
Steven Bright, Vice President of Product Development,
COLDWELL BANKER Real Estate Corporation

Project Manager
George Pelton, Director of Special Markets,
COLDWELL BANKER Real Estate Corporation

Editor/Research Assistant
Sarah W. Stoddard

Desktop Publisher
Jim Uhing, Studio U

Book Jacket Design
The Sawtooth Group, North Woodbridge, NJ

Printing
Merrill Corporation, St. Cloud, MN

Foreword

Have you ever dreamed of owning a vacation property? A seaside condo, an A-frame or condo on the ski slopes, a cabin on the lake, a home or villa at a golf and tennis resort, or perhaps a timeshare at a resort destination?

If so, we invite you to use this book as a road map to realizing that dream. Whether you already own a vacation property or are just beginning to consider the possibilities, this book is for you. Carefully researched, written, and edited, this book contains special information that can help with your decision to purchase a vacation property, or obtain more from your investment after you own one — more rentals, more fun, more value, and more excitement.

My own dream came true in 1981, when my wife and I bought a vacation villa at Kiawah Island, South Carolina. We thoroughly enjoyed our vacation property dream for 16 years. We loved taking walks on the beach, playing tennis, teeing off on world-class golf courses, dining on sumptuous seafood, visiting nearby historic Charleston, and sometimes just plain relaxing with a good book, away from the hectic pace of our day-to-day lives.

Somewhere over the rainbow, skies are blue; And the dreams that you dare to dream really do come true.
— Wizard of Oz

During that 16-year journey, we learned quite a bit about buying and owning vacation property. Looking back on the experience now, I realize with the benefit of hindsight that we didn't always take the most direct route. Often we had to detour around roadblocks. From time to time, we took a wrong turn. Once in a while, we just plain lost our way.

We quickly learned that we could benefit from more rentals to help defray our property expenses and to keep our dream alive. A public relations and marketing professional, I decided to apply what I had learned in my career to enhance my vacation property experience. I outlined several techniques to get more rentals for our vacation home. Over the years, we found many simple, practical, and effective ways "to put heads in beds," as they say in the hotel/motel industry.

We found an outstanding rental management company to manage our property and help obtain rentals. We developed an excellent relationship with them. Using the tactics that we ourselves developed, we then augmented their efforts to find additional renters. For example, during a typical year, our management company might obtain 20 weekly rentals for our property, and we would find an additional 5 or 10 for a total of 25 to 30 weeks. More rental income made our property a much better investment.

Good judgment comes from experience, and a lot of that comes from bad judgment.
— Anonymous

It occurred to me that if these ideas helped **me** obtain more rentals, then they could help **anyone** who owns a vacation property. With that in mind, I wrote and published <u>Maximize Your Resort Property Investment</u>, a book designed to help **owners** get more **renters**. The book, published in 1984, was featured editorially in *Barron's, Business Week, USA Today, Money Magazine,* the *Kiplinger Washington Letter,* as well as in other local and national publications.

The book went through two printings. Copies were sold to property owners from every state in the U.S., as well as from Israel, Mexico, Canada, the Bahamas, and other countries in the Caribbean. The book proved to be of value to many vacation property buyers and owners from wide geographic locations.

Thousands of owners have used the ideas from that book to generate extra dollars in rental income. If an owner obtained just one extra rental week using the information, the book paid for itself many times over.

Like anything worth having, ownership of a vacation property involves effort on the part of the property owner. It involves a commitment of time, energy, and resources. This book outlines dozens of ways to locate more renters for your vacation property. These ideas can help generate thousands of dollars in extra rental income. But you must be willing to do a little work, or all of the good ideas in the world won't help. As Thomas Jefferson once said, the harder I work, the more luck I seem to have.

For example, many timeshare owners have long agreed that the best value of ownership is the opportunity to exchange for vacation weeks with other timeshare owners all around the world. Still, many timeshare owners have never made the effort to explore this avenue.

Just like a job, a relationship, an exercise program, or learning a new skill, the more effort you put into the activity, the greater your return will be.

This book contains virtually all of the information from my first book, plus much, much more. In addition to adding new tips and tactics, with the help of Coldwell Banker Real Estate Corporation, we have broadened the scope of the book significantly, expanding it and updating it for today's market. While the first book helped owners locate more renters, this book begins by helping with your decision about purchasing a vacation property, and then goes on to provide helpful tips and techniques for owners to make the most of their investment — both financially as well as with the enjoyment of the property.

What this book can do for you...

If you are considering the purchase of your own vacation home, a fractional ownership interest in a vacation home, or a timeshare, this book will:

- Help you make an informed buying decision.

If you currently own vacation property, this book will:

- Help you generate thousands of dollars in additional rental revenue.
- Help you get more fun, excitement, and value from your property.

Whether you already own, or are actively exploring the purchase of a vacation property, this book:

- Offers ideas and advice from the country's foremost experts on timeshare, keeping records, furnishing your vacation property, trading vacation properties, and working with your rental manager.
- Contains a wealth of information designed to help you get the most from your timeshare or vacation property.

We've added guest editorials from some of the country's foremost experts — sections on furnishing your vacation property, keeping good tax records, financing your vacation property, and taking a look at timeshares, the fastest growing segment of the vacation property industry. This information comes directly from the experts, the leaders in highly specialized areas that apply to vacation property ownership.

This book also includes valuable directories – information at your fingertips – and special money saving offers to help you get more value out of your vacation property. And speaking of value, we not only improved the product, we lowered the price!

<u>**Road Map to Your Vacation Property Dream**</u> was written and compiled by one who has traveled the road before. It is designed to help you arrive at your dream by a more direct route, using the experience of others to pave the way. This book will help you avoid the pitfalls and discover the hidden treasures of owning a vacation property. It is my hope that it will also add happiness, excitement, and more rental income for those who decide to buy their vacation property dream.

My thanks to Coldwell Banker Real Estate for participating in this project. Of its more than 2700 offices worldwide, more than 800 specialize in vacation property markets (see the directory of Coldwell Banker Resort Property Network™ offices in Section 5 of this book). The brokers and sales associates from Coldwell Banker are *the* experts in vacation property. If you decide to buy a vacation property, they can help turn your dream into a reality while making the process a whole lot easier. Be sure to read the special introduction letter from Alex Perriello, President and CEO of Coldwell Banker Real Estate Corporation, which follows this foreword.

> *Results! Why, man, I have gotten a lot of results. I know several thousand things that won't work.*
> — Thomas A. Edison

According to an ancient Chinese proverb, the longest journey begins with the first step. This book, designed to help you get the most from your vacation property, is the first step to an informed buying decision.

Enjoy the journey to ownership of your vacation property dream!

Christopher S. Cain

Christopher S. Cain
Author, Vacation Property Expert

**A message from Alex Perriello, President and CEO of
COLDWELL BANKER Real Estate Corporation.**

Congratulations on your decision to learn more about purchasing a vacation home property.

Buying a second home is an important investment and **COLDWELL BANKER®** affiliates strive to make the process as simple as possible for you. In the back of this book, you will find a list of more than 800 **COLDWELL BANKER** affiliate offices located in most vacation home markets. With our more than 90 years of real estate experience, we are pleased to offer one comprehensive resource that provides information and tips to help you make a more informed purchase decision.

We hope that this Road Map helps you realize Your Vacation Property Dream.

Best regards,

Alex Perriello

Table of Contents

**Section 4   Maximizing Your Vacation Property Enjoyment:
Remember to Have Fun!**

**Section 5   You're Ready to Buy: Contact the Coldwell Banker
Resort Property Network**

Section 6   Money Saving Resort Property Coupons

Index

Signs

"Sign. Sign. Everywhere a sign. Blocking out the scenery, breaking my mind. Do this! Don't do that! Can't you read the sign?!"
Five Man Electrical Band

Traffic signs are used on the road to keep traffic moving, avoid accidents, and to warn drivers of special conditions or dangers ahead. Here are a few shapes of traffic signs, each with its own precise meaning:

Shape	**Meaning**
Octagon	Stop signs
Horizontal Rectangle	Guide signs
Triangle	Yield signs
Pennant	Advanced warning of no passing zones
Diamond	Warn of existing or possible hazards
Vertical Rectangle	Regulatory signs
Pentagon	School signs
Round	Railroad advanced warnings
Crossbuck	Railroad crossings

Before we begin our journey to your vacation property dream, let's review some of the road signs we may encounter along the way.

Throughout this book, we have used the diamond-shaped caution sign to give you advance notice of potential hazards in buying or owning a vacation property; areas where you should proceed with caution.

Each of these caution signs is followed by a corresponding rectangular guide sign to signify advice, tips, and tactics you can use to avoid delays and detours and to ensure a more pleasant, exciting, and profitable trip.

$\mathcal{W}$HAT TO CONSIDER WHEN BUYING A VACATION PROPERTY

Buy for the Right Reasons

Should you buy a vacation property?

I don't know. Only you can answer that question.

You certainly don't have to. Obviously, it's a luxury and not a necessity. While owning a vacation property can be enriching to your lifestyle, it is not necessarily for everyone.

Do you want to? Can you afford it? Will you enjoy it? These are the real questions.

This book is not meant to advise that you buy a vacation property. That's a personal decision. One you should discuss and decide with your family and perhaps with your accountant, attorney, and/or financial advisor.

Why Buy?

Here are a few reasons why some consumers choose to buy vacation property:

- Fun and enjoyment for their family
- Eventual retirement location
- Real estate investment that may appreciate in value
- Tax shelter
- Opportunity to exchange the use of vacation properties with other owners
- Status

"The road to the City of Emeralds is paved with yellow brick," said the Witch, *"so you cannot miss it. You must walk through a country sometimes pleasant, sometimes dark and terrible."*
— Frank Baum, The Wonderful Wizard of Oz

The American Resort Development Association (ARDA) has done extensive research on the reasons people buy timeshares. (For more information, please see the guest editorial on timeshares by Steve Miller of Resort Condominiums International (RCI) in Section 2 of this book.)

And I can give you my own personal reasons for having bought a vacation property:

- My wife and I fell in love with the area.
- We wanted to own and enjoy a vacation property.
- We thought it would appreciate in value over time.
- We have considered the resort as a retirement possibility.

Of these, we found that the most valid reason we had for purchasing our vacation property was pure enjoyment of ownership. And enjoy it we did. We have fond memories etched in our minds by the wind, sand, sun, and surf. Recollections to last a lifetime.

In another moment, down the rabbit hole went Alice after the White Rabbit, never once considering how in the world she was to get out of it again.
— Lewis Carroll, Alice in Wonderland

Sun and Surf

We bought our seaside hideaway in the South Carolina Low Country in 1981, selling it in 1997 after moving to Orlando, which is only one hour from the seashore.

For 16 years, we traveled from our various homes in Pittsburgh, PA, Columbia, MD, and then Orlando, FL to our home away from home at Kiawah. Different cities. Different jobs. New friends. But through it all, we had our special getaway where we could recharge, relax, and gain perspective. Always upon arriving on the Island, we would walk over the wooden trestles that protect the sand dunes from erosion to the ocean, and we would gaze out at the sea and up and down the 10-mile beach. We were home again.

Over the years, we dined in style at many local restaurants. We golfed on the world-famous course that was the site of the 1991 Ryder Cup. We played tennis on manicured composition courts. At one of the island's favorite haunts, we enjoyed outdoor oyster roasts which featured steamed oysters by the shovelful against a background of foot-stomping bluegrass music.

We soaked up the local history of this proud resort area, and we paid a visit to the location where the Civil War began at 4:30 a.m. on April 12, 1861. We sipped Tennessee sour mash whiskey at the rooftop bar of a local inn and watched the sun set slowly over the city.

We frolicked in the surf with family and friends. We took moonlit walks on the beach. We ventured into the cold, windy night across the wooden walkway and listened to the thunder and watched the lightning of storms raging offshore.

And always it was back to long, solitary, barefoot walks down the sun-drenched beach. Feeling the tensions and anxieties melt away. Watching brown pelicans fly in perfect formation just 30 feet above the ground.

While my wife and I selected the low country of the Carolinas for our vacation property dream, everyone has personal preferences.

Action and Adventure

You may dream of action-packed vacations. You buy a chalet on the ski slopes where you rise at daybreak to catch the first lift up the mountain. On the chair lift to the summit, you discover an overnight snow storm has sprinkled four inches of fresh powder on the mountain. With the sun rising in the Rockies, you ski down the slopes through a pristine winter wonderland.

Bone tired by four that afternoon, you return to your chalet for a shower, change of clothes, and a short nap. Then you head to the lodge for a massage to work out some kinks and soothe some sore muscles.

Back at the chalet, your friends show up about 7 p.m. for wine and cheese before you all head out for dinner at a new restaurant in town.

Later, if you can believe it, you try line dancing at a country-western bar and sample some of the micro-brewed malt beverages. You even manage to renew an old acquaintance with Jose Cuervo. Which could explain the slight headache as you head up the slopes at daybreak only five hours later!

Time for Some R&R

Perhaps you dream of a peaceful cabin on the lake. Instead of exercise and constant activity, your dream is rest, recuperation, and relaxation. Your vacation property affords a slow-paced return to nature, deep in the woods.

You read on your porch. Play cards long into the evening. Fish for hours, never minding for a minute that nothing is nibbling at the hook. You watch the steam rise from the lake as the loons dive for fish. You meander down a hiking trail, stopping often to focus your binoculars on yet another bird in the forest canopy.

What will you do tomorrow? You can decide that when you wake up.

Passion for Golf

Or perhaps you dream of combining your passion for golf with owning a vacation condo at a golf resort. You pick a resort with fine golf courses and with many others nearby. You select a new condo overlooking the 14th fairway. You get to know the pro at the club. During each vacation to your condo, you take a lesson. You make an effort to improve your game. You practice. You play. And you play some more. You try many of the area's challenging courses and return to play your favorites again. Your condo provides guaranteed accommodations whenever you want to plan a golf getaway. You're not a visitor to this golf area, you're an owner.

The Financial Aspect

We appreciated every moment at our property. In our case, as it turns out, this was the most rewarding part of our investment.

Financially, our vacation property did not appreciate in value at the rate we had hoped for. In fact, it appreciated very little. For us, there were extenuating circumstances with the location, the economy, population demographics, and federal policy that caused our property to go up in value during some years, and down in value during others.

Still, during this same period of time, there were other vacation property owners who reaped sizable profits when they sold their properties.

Vacation properties in some locations have doubled and tripled in value since 1981. Mountains, oceans, rivers, and lakes are limited resources, so property on or near these resources is more likely to gain in value. It can and it does happen. The value of location and doing your homework can not be emphasized strongly enough if financial rewards are an important part of your vacation property buying decision.

Also to consider, vacation properties come with their own set of expenses (mortgage, taxes, insurance, utilities, upkeep, etc.). You may be able to write off a portion of these expenses (see your accountant for specifics on deduction eligibility). And you may be able to recoup much of your costs by renting out your vacation property (see Section 3 for tips and techniques for getting extra rentals). But, let's face it, from a strictly financial perspective, a vacation property is not a sure thing.

However, as Oliver Wendell Homes, Jr. once put it, life is painting a picture, not doing a sum. You might find better investments – outlets that will earn more for your initial investment dollar. But let's consider the intangible benefits: years of holiday enjoyment for you, your friends, and family; a place that is familiar, yet outside the realm of the day-to-day; your own little getaway. After all, man does not live by bread alone.

Recommendation

My recommendation, if you will take a piece of advice from someone who has been there and done that...someone who has seen the ups and downs of the vacation property experience:

Don't buy vacation property as an investment. If it appreciates in value, that's fine. That's a bonus. But investment potential should not be your primary reason for purchasing. **Buy the property because you truly want to own it.** Buy it because you want to spend your vacations there. Buy it because you, your family, and your friends will enjoy it.

At the time of this writing, the economy is strong, inflation is low, interest rates are below 7 percent for a 30-year, fixed-rate mortgage, and an onset of great demand for vacation property ownership is about to hit (see Chapter 2, Here Come the Boomers). Now may be one of the best times in history to buy a vacation property.

Action Steps

 As with any major purchase, make an informed buying decision.

 Buy a vacation property because you want to own and enjoy it.

 Don't buy vacation property primarily as an investment.

Here Come the Boomers

In the next hour, 488 Americans will turn 50. Today, 11,720 baby boomers will turn 50. This month, 356,481 middle-aged consumers will turn 50. This year, 4.27 million people in America hit the big 5-Oh! And, an average of 4.27 million people will reach 50 for each of the next 16 years, just as they have for the past 2 years!

The same folks who marched on Washington in protest of a war and frolicked in the mud at Woodstock are now teachers, doctors, lawyers, and yes, in some cases, even grandparents.

Baby boomers, the generation of people born between the years of 1946 and 1964, includes about 77 million adults in their most productive years. That represents one-third of the total U.S. population. By the year 2020, the baby boomer generation will represent fully one-half of the total U.S. population. Add to that the 9 million Canadian baby boomers.

I have some personal perspective on the baby boomers, because I am the oldest baby boomer in the country. I was born in 1946 and I graduated from high school in 1964, the year the boom went bust. To be totally honest, I am not actually the oldest. I was born in early February, 1946, so there are about 400,000 baby boomers who are older than me.

Why make such a big deal about the boomers?

What is my point? The point is, that baby boomers constitute the largest group of consumers in the nation. According to the American Resort Development Association (ARDA), householders in their late 40s to early 50s are the most affluent group and the biggest spenders. At this age, people are not quite ready for retirement, but they no longer have the financial burden of kids in school. This is the age at which Americans are most likely to buy a vacation property.

One observer characterized the baby boomers as the "pig in the belly of the python." This huge market of 77 million consumers will play a key role in vacation property, just as they will have a major impact on most other aspects of our economy. For the next two decades, owners, sellers, developers, sales agents, planners, designers, and others involved in vacation property will experience a golden age as the "pig" works its way through the system. The baby boomers may well cause a new real estate boom.

The Boomer Market

As the baby boomers turn 50, they cross what has traditionally been the threshold into the "mature market." Market analysts agree, however, that rather than join the traditional mature market, boomers will create a new and vibrant mid-life marketplace, reflecting their own unique attitudes and lifestyles. Increased educational level, working women, divorce, individualistic attitudes, small families, and dual incomes all combine to create a new consumer market.

After years of working hard, with mounting responsibilities and a heavy sense of duty and obligation, boomers are eager to get back to "doing their own thing." They want to do something for themselves. During the mid-life years, job and family responsibilities mount, leading to mid-life

> *Setting a good example for children takes all the fun out of middle age.*
> — William Feather

crises, usually revolving around family, job, and/or health. With so much responsibility, life's excitement wanes. Boomers are looking for adventure, for ways to escape the tedium. Having gotten beyond family obligations, boomers think it's time to go out and have some fun.

With 77 million people entering this period of their lives in the next 16 years, at least a few million of them will have the financial capability to buy real estate in a resort market. And several million more will be interested in vacationing there.

According to Cheryl Russell in her book <u>100 Predictions for the Baby Boom: The Next 50 Years</u>, spending on vacation homes and hotels will be one of the most rapidly growing expenditure categories in the next few decades because the baby boomers will travel more and in more style.

What Are the Boomers Like?

Boomers are well-educated. Among the oldest baby boomers, fully 87 percent are high school graduates. More than one in four are college graduates, and over half have some college experience. This makes them more demanding, more sophisticated consumers than the previous generation, many of whom did not have a high school diploma.

Boomers are also highly individualistic, which translates into highly independent and self-indulgent consumer patterns. Boomers are willing to try new things and pay top dollar if they feel they are getting good value.

A substantial number of older baby boom couples have had a dual-earner household for decades. Not known for their thriftiness, boomers entering the empty nest stage of their lives will probably see a dramatic change in their spending habits. They may will be interested in buying property in resort communities for investment purposes.

What are the Boomers Looking For?

When looking to buy (or rent) property, boomers are interested in cultural amenities (concerts, theater, lectures, etc.) as well as outdoor sports (golf, tennis, skiing, etc.). They're interested in a certain lifestyle, a sense of community. Emphasis will be placed on fun, comfort, and personal health.

Boomers are looking for products and services that will help them secure their future, save them time, lower their hassle factor, and/or improve their quality of life. With proper management, property ownership in a resort community can address all of these.

Action Steps:

 Baby boomers, by their sheer number, will create a huge demand for vacation property over the next two decades. The best time to buy is *before* this huge demand has caused an increase in vacation property prices.

True Vacation Value

When weighing the pros and cons of owning a vacation property, put value, fun, and excitement at the top of your "pros" list. And that is value, fun, and excitement not just for you and your family, but also for anyone who might rent your property from you for their family vacation. Vacationers will find a "home away from home" with all the privacy and convenience they expect.

If you buy a vacation property, assess your purchase. It represents a highly marketable and highly rentable commodity.

Consider the vacation options: a resort hotel room, a cramped cabin on a cruise, or a privately-owned vacation house or condo at the destination of your choice.

Count the following among the many advantages a privately-owned vacation property has over a resort hotel room:

Savings on Meals – A furnished kitchen allows vacationers to prepare many of their own meals. During a week's vacation, dining in, rather than going to restaurants for every meal translates into several hundred dollars in savings on food alone.

More Room – A vacation home, condo, or villa usually has more space than a resort hotel room. Often, the condo or villa has a living room, dining room, kitchen, and perhaps a porch, balcony, or deck. When you're on vacation, it's nice to have some space.

Beautiful Furnishings – Many vacation properties reflect the good taste and pride of the owners with fine furnishings and decorator touches.

More Privacy – Often the homes, villas, and condos are more secluded, more private than a room in a hotel. In a resort hotel, you may have revelers roaming the halls at all hours.

Fully Equipped – In addition to a furnished kitchen with microwave and refrigerator, the vacation property may have a washer and dryer. Guests can wash their golf, tennis, ski, or beach wear each day. Hidden benefit: less luggage to haul on the trip.

Mini Bar vs. Refrigerator – Take a single beer from the hotel mini-bar or take a six-pack from the refrigerator at the condo. Guess what? The cost is about the same. Mini-bars provide great profit centers for hotels. Refrigerators, microwaves, VCRs, washers and dryers provide excellent convenience and savings for vacationers.

Tales From the Road...

We planned dinner for five...so we ordered four pounds of large shrimp from Bohicket Marina, located just outside the entrance to Kiawah Island, SC. Kiawah, a 10,000-acre barrier island resort, is located 20 miles south of historic Charleston and we were vacationing at our seaside villa.

You must order your shrimp before noon, then pick it up when the shrimp boats come in around 4:00 p.m. During that day, on our long walks on the 10-mile beach and our frolics in the ocean surf, we watched the shrimp boats a mile or so offshore, followed by flocks of seagulls. Those fishermen were catching our dinner.

After picking up the shrimp at the marina, we returned to our vacation villa. We lightly sautéed the shrimp with butter, a splash of Chardonnay, and freshly pressed garlic, then served it with brown rice, and a fresh garden salad. For dessert, we had a fresh fruit medley (strawberries, mango, and kiwifruit) and some aged cheddar cheese with crackers, followed by coffee. A simple, yet elegant dinner.

In our many trips to Kiawah, we have dined at many of the area's wonderful restaurants: the Jasmine Porch, Roberts of Charleston, 82 Queen, The Colony House, The Privateer, and Carolina's to name a few. But, for fun, freshness, ambiance, and taste, that shrimp dinner at our villa ranks as one of our finest dining experiences in the Charleston area.

As for value: When we stopped to compare with the cost of feeding five at a fine restaurant, we conservatively calculated our savings at about $200. Had we vacationed in a hotel room, we would not have been able to experience this dining delight.

Better Rates – Despite these many advantages, privately-owned vacation property often costs less per week or per day than a hotel room at the same resort.

Finding a Vacation Property to Rent

So, where do you find a piece of paradise to rent?

According to the Ragatz Associates study, <u>The American Recreational Property Survey: 1990</u>, there's an ample supply of vacation properties to choose from: "6.3 million recreational properties of all types within the 50 United States...About 4.6 million of these are living units of some type, primarily vacation homes, cabins, and condominiums (both time-share and whole ownership)."

Check out the classified section of your newspaper under "Vacation Properties," "Vacation Rentals," "Beach Rentals," or a similar category. Magazines such as *Sunset, Midwest Life,* and *Southern Living* feature display ads and hundreds of classifieds representing thousands of properties. City magazines usually feature vacation classifieds and display ads.

Check newsletters at your job and in your community. Bulletin boards at work, at the grocery store, at church, at community centers often display ads for private vacation property. Your friends, neighbors, and business associates might have vacation properties you could rent.

Contact one of the Resort Property Network™ offices for Coldwell Banker found in Section 5.

The Vacation Rental Managers Association (VRMA) represents about 200 rental managers throughout the U.S. and Canada. For a free directory of rental properties across the U.S., visit their Web site at http://www.vrma.com or call 1-800-871-8762.

Value is the life-giving power of anything.
— John Ruskin

Check out the Internet. More than 4000 Web sites showcase real estate, including vacation property. Search using "vacation rentals," "beachfront property," "Florida vacation rentals," or similar keywords.

Also be sure to visit the award-winning Web site for Coldwell Banker where you'll find a special section for resort and vacation properties. The address is www.coldwellbanker.com.

Privately-owned property can be your passport to an exciting, fun-filled, and affordable vacation. You're sure to come home relaxed and refreshed. Along with the many wonderful vacation memories, you just might find you came home with some savings in your pocket! Those are the best vacations of all.

Action Steps:

Be sure to consider the value, fun, and excitement of a privately-owned vacation property over other types of vacation accommodations.

A vacation property represents a valuable and highly marketable commodity offering true value to renters.

The American Dream

The American Dream, as it pertains to vacation property, goes something like this:

You buy a vacation property at the seashore (or on the ski slopes, at the desert or at the lake). You and your family vacation at your private hideaway for two weeks each year. The rest of the year, you rent it to other vacationers and the rental income pays all the expenses.

Over the years, the property appreciates in value. You sell it at a pretty profit to augment your retirement income. Or you sell your primary residence and retire to your vacation property. Or you leave it to your children in your will so that future generations can share the enjoyment of your private paradise.

Is this dream possible? Yes.

Plausible? Perhaps.

Practical? You can make most of it happen. However, some factors are beyond your control. No one can foresee war, recession, inflation, or natural disasters that could impact your property. (Please note that these factors can also impact other types of investments such as stocks, mutual funds, and bonds.) Legislation can also affect your property value. While the Economic Recovery Act of 1981 encouraged buying vacation property with many tax incentives, the Tax Reform Act of 1986 reduced incentives. The pendulum has again swung in a favorable direction with the Tax Payer Relief Act of 1997. This legislation reduces capital gains tax from 28 percent to various lower rates.

Fortune assists the bold.
— Virgil

On the other hand, you can control many of the factors that affect your property. When considering a purchase, the more sophisticated vacation property buyer will ask the real estate sales agent, "Will I have a positive cash flow?" In other words, will my rental income cover my expenses?

A good real estate agent will not answer this question. First, many state real estate commissions or regulatory bodies prohibit sales agents from promising or guaranteeing you a certain amount of rentals. How can they? Second, even if they had a general idea of the rental income you might expect (who can predict the future?), they would also have to know your actual property expenses which can vary dramatically.

To illustrate the point, let's take a look at two highly simplified property budgets.

Note that Owner A has a higher mortgage payment. Also note that the low rental income does not cover Owner A's monthly expenses. Owner A has a net average loss each month of $400, the difference between monthly expenses and average monthly rental income.

Monthly Expenses		
	Owner A	Owner B
Mortgage	$1200	$ 800
Taxes	100	100
Utilities	100	100
Maintenance	200	200
Management	200	300
Total Expenses	**$1800**	**$1500**
Rental Income	$1400	$2100

Owner B has a positive cash flow of $600 each month. The difference? Owner B has a lower monthly mortgage payment (probably the result of a much larger down payment on the property). Also, Owner B gets one third more rentals than Owner A.

Other than that, their expenses are the same, except that Owner B pays $300 a month rather than $200 a month for management because the rental management company takes a commission on the additional one third rentals.

Grant me the courage to change the things I can control, the ability to accept the things I cannot control, and the wisdom to know the difference.
— Anonymous

While this is a very simplified example, you can see that the two major variables in the positive cash flow equation are: mortgage payment and rental income. You have control over both of these.

15

Your mortgage payments will reflect your down payment, the interest rate, and the type of mortgage product you select (15-year, fixed-rate; 30-year, adjustable-rate; etc.). Remember that if you select an adjustable-rate mortgage, your monthly payments could go up or down in the future to reflect prevailing interest rates.

Whatever you can do or dream you can, begin it. Boldness has genius, power and magic in it.
— Goethe

For ideas on how to increase your rental income, see Section 3 of this book. In that section, we outline tips and tactics to help you locate renters for your vacation property. These ideas for putting "heads in beds" can help you put thousands of dollars of extra rental income in your pocket.

Action Steps:

 Budget before you buy. Get advice from your accountant. See article in Section 2 of this book by Valerie Terry, Director of Jackson Hewitt Tax Service.

 Choose a mortgage product and interest rate that will keep your mortgage payment in an affordable range. See article in Section 2 of this book by Terry Edwards, president and CEO of Cendant Mortgage.

 Work with your rental manager to secure rentals.

 See Section 3 of this book for tips and tactics to secure additional rentals over and above those your rental management company finds for you.

Vacation Property Expenses

– Take a Look at Schedule E

A vacation homeowner who meets certain tests based on the days of rental and personal usage may deduct expenses and losses (expenses in excess of income). See your accountant for specifics on your deduction eligibility.

Generally speaking, however, if you use your vacation property as a second home and do not rent it, or if you rent it less than 14 days per year, you do not have to report any rental income. You can deduct your mortgage interest and real estate taxes.

> *In this world, nothing is certain but death and taxes.*
>
> — Benjamin Franklin

If you rent your vacation property for more than 14 days, you will report income and expenses to the Internal Revenue Service on Schedule E. Take a look at this form below. It gives you a complete picture of the categories of expenses you will encounter with your vacation property.

Action Steps

 Take a look at Schedule E before you buy vacation property.

 Develop a plan with your accountant on the best way to save your receipts, and record and report all vacation property related expenses.

 See the article on record keeping by Valerie Terry in Section 2 of this book.

SCHEDULE E	**Supplemental Income and Loss**	OMB No. 1545–0074
(Form 1040)	(From rental real estate, royalties, partnerships, S corporations, estates, trusts, REMICs, etc.)	**1997**
Department of the Treasury Internal Revenue Service (99)	▶ **Attach to Form 1040 or Form 1041.** ▶ **See Instructions for Schedule E (Form 1040).**	Attachment Sequence No. **13**
Name(s) shown on return		Your social security no.

Part I **Income or Loss From Rental Real Estate and Royalties** Note: Report income and expenses from your business of renting personal property on **Schedule C** or **C–EZ** (see page E–1). Report farm rental income or loss from **Form 4835** on page 2, line 39.

1	Show the kind and location of each **rental real estate property:**	2 For each rental real estate property listed on line 1, did you or your family use it during the tax year for personal purposes more than the greater of: • 14 days, or • 10% of the total days rented at fair rental value? (See page E–1.)	Yes	No
A		A		
B		B		
C		C		

Income:		Properties			Totals
		A	B	C	(Add columns A, B, and C.)
3 Rents received	3				3
4 Royalties received	4				4
Expenses:					
5 Advertising	5				
6 Auto and travel (see page E–2)	6				
7 Cleaning and maintenance	7				
8 Commissions	8				
9 Insurance	9				
10 Legal and other professional fees	10				
11 Management fees	11				
12 Mortgage interest paid to banks, etc. (see page E–2)	12				12
13 Other interest	13				
14 Repairs	14				
15 Supplies	15				
16 Taxes	16				
17 Utilities	17				
18 Other (list) ▶	18				
19 Add lines 5 through 18	19				19
20 Depreciation expense or depletion (see page E–2)	20				20
21 Total expenses. Add lines 19 and 20	21				
22 Income or (loss) from rental real estate or royalty properties. Subtract line 21 from line 3 (rents) or line 4 (royalties). If the result is a (loss), see page E–3 to find out if you must file **Form 6198**	22				
23 Deductible rental real estate loss. **Caution:** Your rental real estate loss on line 22 may be limited. See page E–3 to find out if you must file **Form 8582.** Real estate professionals must complete line 42 on page 2	23	(	)(	)(	)

24 **Income.** Add positive amounts shown on line 22. **Do not** include any losses	24	
25 **Losses.** Add royalty losses from line 22 and rental real estate losses from line 23. Enter total losses here	25	( )
26 Total rental real estate and royalty income or (loss). Combine lines 24 and 25. Enter the result here. If Parts II, III, IV, and line 39 on page 2 do not apply to you, also enter this amount on Form 1040, line 17. Otherwise, include this amount in the total on line 40 on page 2	26	

For **Paperwork Reduction Act Notice, see Form 1040 Inst.**   CAA   7   E12   NTF 11077   Prepares Edition **Schedule E (Form 1040) 1997**
Copyright Forms Software Only, 1997 Nelco, Inc.

Schedule E (Form 1040) 1997   Attachment Sequence No. **13**   Page **2**

Name(s) shown on return. Do not enter name and social security number if shown on other side.   **Your social security no.**

Note: If you report amounts from farming or fishing on Schedule E, you must enter your gross income from those activities on line 41 below. Real estate professionals must complete line 42 below.

Part II   **Income or Loss From Partnerships and S Corps. Note:** If you report a loss from an at-risk activity, you MUST check either col. **(e)** or **(f)** on line 27 to describe your investment in activity. See page E-4. If you check col. **(f)**, you must attach **Form 6198.**

27 (a) Name	(b) Enter P for partnership; S for S corp.	(c) Check if foreign partnership	(d) Employer identification number	Investment At Risk? (e) All is at risk	(f) Some is not at risk
A					
B					
C					
D					
E					

Passive Income and Loss		Nonpassive Income and Loss		
(g) Passive loss allowed (attach **Form 8582** if required)	(h) Passive income from **Schedule K-1**	(I) Nonpassive loss from **Schedule K-1**	(J) Section 179 expense deduction from **Form 4562**	(k) Nonpassive income from **Schedule K-1**
A				
B				
C				
D				
E				
28a Totals				
b Totals				

29	Add columns (h) and (k) of line 28a	29	
30	Add columns (g), (i), and (j) of line 28b	30 (	)
31	Total partnership and S corporation income or (loss). Combine lines 29 and 30. Enter the result here and include in the total on line 40 below	31	

Part III   **Income or Loss From Estates and Trusts**

32 (a) Name	(b) Employer identification number
A	
B	

Passive Income and Loss		Nonpassive Income and Loss	
(c) Passive deduction or loss allowed (attach **Form 8582** if required)	(d) Passive income from **Schedule K-1**	(e) Deduction or loss from **Schedule K-1**	(f) Other income from **Schedule K-1**
A			
B			
33a Totals			
b Totals			

34	Add columns (d) and (f) of line 33a.	34	
35	Add columns (c) and (e) of line 33b	35 (	)
36	Total estate and trust income or (loss). Combine lines 34 and 35. Enter the result here and include in the total on line 40 below	36	

Part IV   **Income or Loss From Real Estate Mortgage Investment Conduits (REMICs) --- Residual Holder**

37 (a) Name	(b) Employer identification number	(c) Excess inclusion from **Schedules Q**, line 2c (see page E-5)	(d) Taxable income (net loss) from **Schedules Q**, line 1b	(e) Income from **Schedules Q**, line 3b

| 38 | Combine columns (d) and (e) only. Enter the result here and include in the total on line 40 below . . . . | 38 | |

Part V   **Summary**

39	Net farm rental income or (loss) from **Form 4835.** Also, complete line 41 below.	39	
40	TOTAL income or (loss). Combine lines 26, 31, 36, 38, & 39. Enter the result here and on Form 1040, line 17▶	40	
41	**Reconciliation of Farming and Fishing Income.** Enter your **gross** farming and fishing income reported on Form 4835, line 7; Schedule K-1 (Form 1065), line 15b; Schedule K-1 (Form 1120S), line 23; and Schedule K-1 (Form 1041), line 14 (see page E-5)	41	
42	**Reconciliation for Real Estate Professionals.** If you were a real estate professional (see page E-4), enter the net income or (loss) you reported anywhere on Form 1040 from all rental real estate activities in which you materially participated under the passive activity loss rules	42	

CAA   **7**   **E12**   NTF 11078
Copyright Forms Software Only, 1997 Nelco, Inc.

19

WHAT THE EXPERTS HAVE TO SAY

The Power of Partners

Two hikers in Yellowstone National Park in Wyoming surprised a foraging grizzly bear that began to chase them. As they fled, one hiker said to the other, "We must be crazy. There's no way we can outrun a grizzly!" The other hiker (now turned sprinter) replied, "I know I can't outrun a grizzly. I only have to outrun you!"

This "bear in the woods" joke provides a good analogy to much of today's business world:

The bear represents the uncertainties and danger of the marketplace, such as labor shortages and strikes, high inflation, high interest rates, recession, government regulation, environmental regulation, and other factors that can adversely impact business.

The hikers represent competition – in this case a life and death competition – among similar businesses.

As the joke illustrates, business can be cutthroat, competition can be fierce.

Rather than compete, some businesses are finding it's better to cooperate.

Some years ago, I approached Coldwell Banker Real Estate Corporation (Coldwell Banker) to discuss this book project. I sought guidance from Coldwell Banker because my research indicated they were the experts in vacation property.

On a trip to meet with several Coldwell Banker executives to discuss our book, I flew to Newark, NJ and rented a car for the drive to Coldwell Banker headquarters in Parsippany. At the start of our meeting, I mentioned that I had tried to rent an Avis rental car. I knew that Avis, like Coldwell Banker, was owned by the HFS Corporation. I wanted to rent the Avis car because it would keep all the revenue under the HFS umbrella.

"Unfortunately," I told the executives, "Avis had rented its entire fleet that day and I had to rent a car from Alamo instead."

"That's all right," one of them replied. "Actually," he explained, "we don't own them. They are an HFS preferred alliance partner."

Since then, HFS merged with CUC in 1997 to form a new company called Cendant Corporation. Cendant has engineered a corporation that develops and builds business relationships. The Cendant Corporation promotes alliances, cooperation, and synergy among its many fine companies, including Resort Condominiums International (RCI), the world's largest timeshare exchange company; Ramada; Days Inn; Avis; ERA; Coldwell Banker; Century 21; and CUC with its vast consumer database and programs, including Travel Advantage and Auto Vantage. Cendant's success testifies to the power of partners.

This section of the book puts the power of several Cendant partners to work for you. For information on financing your vacation property, we enlisted the help of Terry Edwards, president and CEO of Cendant Mortgage Company. Valerie Terry, Director of Jackson Hewitt Tax Service, authored our article on accounting and record keeping. For tips on timeshare, who could be more qualified to provide valuable information than Steve Miller, chief executive officer of RCI?

Finally, my thanks to Ken Ratcliffe, president of Orlando-based Seltar Interiors, for his guest editorial on furnishing a vacation property. If only I could have read Ken's article before we furnished our condo! His information would have saved us several wrong turns and detours in furnishing our property.

The only thing one can do with good advice is to pass it on. It is never of any use to oneself.
— Oscar Wilde

Before we move on to the guest editorials, let's return for a moment to the bear in the woods story. If the hikers were to concentrate on cooperation rather than competition, they would not engage in a life and death foot race, with the loser falling prey to the bear. Rather, they would work together to thwart the bear. Perhaps one could create a distraction, giving the other one time to find food in his backpack and throw it to the bear. Or maybe they could start a fire, or form a united front and scream or bang sticks together. Or maybe they would both play dead until the bear returned to its foraging. The point is, they could work together to ensure their mutual survival.

Action Step:

 "Bear in mind," cooperation is often more productive than competition.

 Spend time with the experts for insights and information on financing, accounting, timeshare demographics, vacation property exchange, and interior design.

Financing a Vacation Property

by Terry Edwards

Terry Edwards is the president and chief executive officer of Cendant Mortgage, a subsidiary of Cendant Corporation. For more information about Cendant Mortgage and how they can help you finance your vacation property, call 1-888-CBHOME4.

I am a baby boomer. I am married with three children, ages 19, 16, and 11. For the past five years, we have owned a second home in the mountains of Pennsylvania, where I have vacationed every year of my life. That said, I would like to offer my thoughts on purchasing a second home.

My thoughts are divided into nine different categories. However, the common need for anyone buying a home of any kind is to work with people you can trust. This is especially important when it comes to a second home, because you are typically completing the transaction long distance.

1) Emotions – You are making an investment. This may be the house of your dreams or the location of your dreams, but don't let emotions get in the way when it comes to negotiating the price. Since you have made it this far, it is not inconceivable that you will want to buy a bigger second home in five to 10 years.

2) Condominiums – Make sure Fannie Mae (Federal National Mortgage Association) and Freddie Mac (Federal Home Loan Mortgage Corporation) have approved the development for financing. These two financial institutions are the source for the most popular financing in the country and they review all condominium projects. This is where most banks and mortgage companies get their funds and without this financing, you may pay a higher interest rate on your loan and the lack of this financing in the future could affect the value of your investment.

25

3) **Children** – If you have kids, your kids will not view the second home as you do. This will be a function of their ages and what entertainment is available. Make sure there are other children available for your children to interact with.

4) **Mortgage Rates** – In the past, rates for second homes were higher than rates for primary homes. This was because if borrowers encountered financial problems, they would most likely stop making the payments on the second home before they stopped paying on the primary home. This is no longer true; like other national lenders, we provide the same rates for second homes as they do for primary homes.

5) **Pre-Approval** – Get pre-approved for a mortgage before you look at homes, as this will improve your negotiating position. To be competitive, we guarantee same-day loan decisions for all of our customers (or we pay them $250), enabling them to act quickly with favorable negotiating power when they find the "right" property. Because you are dealing long distance, make sure you are working with a reliable lender with a successful track record.

6) **Cash Required to Close** – In our case, we provide a Good Faith Estimate to tell our customers approximately how much cash will be required to purchase their second home. This provides peace of mind while minimizing unpleasant surprises down the road when it comes time to conclude their purchase.

> *Money is better than poverty, if only for financial reasons.*
> — Woody Allen

7) **What kind of mortgage is the best type for a vacation property?** – There are a variety of programs that allow customers to purchase vacation properties as second homes or as investment properties: fixed-rate, adjustable-rate, balloon, etc. For your convenience, a definition of each of these products is provided below. Your mortgage consultant will help you find the option that best suits your specific needs.

However, because of the stability it offers, a 30-year fixed-rate mortgage is an excellent option. A fixed-rate mortgage ensures that your principal and interest payment will never change for the life of the loan. In addition, a fixed-rate mortgage calls for a 10 percent down payment, while adjustable rate and balloon mortgages typically require a 20 percent down payment. For example: On a 30 year fixed mortgage of $125,00 with a 7% interest, zero points, and a 10% down payment, your APR (annual percentage rate) would be 7.57% (including 15 days of per diem interest and fees for tax service, flood certification, application, credit report, appraisal and private mortgage insurance) and your monthly payment would be $885.79. That's quite a big difference in funds.

The amount of interest paid over the life of the loan is more a function of the term than the rate. If paying the loan quicker is a goal, you can make additional payments each month to pay off the loan before the end of 30 years. However, if there is a month when cash is needed for other uses, you can always make the regular 30-year payment.

An adjustable-rate mortgage does offer some advantages: 1) lower *initial* payment, 2) easier to qualify for than fixed-rate, and 3) ability to take advantage of declining interest rates during each cycle. Then again, interest rates may not decline. In fact, they could go up.

If I were advising my brother (or any customer for that matter), I would ask one question: "Will you be living in the property for more than 3 years?" If he answers, "Yes," I strongly suggest a fixed-rate loan. If he answers, "No," I discuss the specifics of the transaction, keeping in mind that fixed-rate loans (including hybrid fixed-rate loans) are currently at very low levels.

8) Vacation Home – Also remember that having a vacation home requires that you do work that you normally don't do when you are on vacation. For instance, you will have to mow your lawn, paint and perform other maintenance functions. It will be unlike most vacations you have had in the past.

9) Considerations When Purchasing a Timeshare – Should you take out a home equity loan to purchase a timeshare? The mortgage interest deduction is an attractive consideration when deciding to finance any major purchase with deductible mortgage interest versus non-deductible cosumer loan interest. Your mortgage consultant can provide a detailed cost comparison between using a first mortgage program or a home equity product to finance a timeshare or any other major purchase.

Mortgage Term Definitions

Fixed-Rate – Mortgages with constant interest rates that will not change over the life of the loan. Fixed-rate loans are typically available with a payback period of either 15 or 30 years. A fixed-rate 15-year term loan, for example, might have a lower interest rate than a 30-year term loan, but the monthly payments are higher because the principal is being paid off twice as fast. With this type of loan, principal and interest payments never rise, regardless of inflation.

Balloon – This is a short-term loan, usually at a fixed rate, paid back in equal monthly payments and a final "balloon" payment for the remaining balance. You enjoy full tax benefits and a lower monthly payment, but there is less equity build-up. Finally, the balloon payment usually requires refinancing or selling the house.

Adjustable-Rate Mortgages (ARM) – Mortgages with interest rates that change at preset intervals, ranging from every six months to every five years, but the most common adjustment is made annually on the anniversary date of the loan's first payment date. Lenders peg the interest rates they charge for adjustable loans to an independent short-term financial index, such as the Treasury Bill. Although adjustables provide an affordable way to buy a home when fixed rates are high, there is an inherent risk to the consumer of paying a higher rate of interest and higher monthly payments in the future.

Adjustable-Rate Cap – To protect consumers from large rate increases, most lenders set limits on the amount rates may fluctuate when it is time for a loan's interest rate to be adjusted. Most lenders cap rate increases and decreases at 2 percentage points per year.

Lifetime Cap - In addition to caps on individual adjustments, most lenders set a ceiling and floor for rate increases and decreases over the life of an adjustable loan. The lifetime cap is expressed either as a particular percentage rate or as 5 to 7 percentage points over or under the initial rate. Ask the lender to explain the lifetime cap thoroughly.

Margin Over Index – Margins are a key factor in comparison shopping for adjustable-rate loans. Lenders adjust interest rates by adding the margin to the loan index, which provides the base rate. For example, say a borrower's initial rate is 9 percent. At adjustment time, the lender's index is 7.87 percent. The margin is 2.5 percent. The borrower's new interest rate, therefore is 10.37 percent, the sum of 7.87 and 2.5. The margin represents extra interest charged by the lender to cover expenses.

Points – The lender's upfront fee, expressed as percentage points on the amount borrowed. A point is also called a discount fee. This fee covers a discount paid by mortgage companies to institutional lenders when the companies sell mortgage-backed securities in order to raise money to lend to home buyers. Points can vary from lender to lender and can be used as a competitive feature in a mortgage deal. Because points are considered a prepayment of interest, they are tax deductible for the year in which they are paid, provided the points are not deducted from the loan proceeds.

Annual Percentage Rates – Lenders calculate annual percentage rates using a government-set criteria that reflects the basic interest rate as well as certain fees for originating, processing, and closing a loan. Lenders are required to disclose it to the borrower within 72 hours or three business days after the application is made.

Locked-In Rate – When the lender has approved the mortgage application and issues a formal commitment to lend a specific amount at a specific rate of interest. Usually, a locked-in rate is guaranteed for a specified time period up to the closing. And the lender will honor the rate stated within that time period. Borrowers should be certain they understand the rate commitment and the time it is to remain in effect.

Loan Limits – Consumers shopping for the "best" interest rate should be aware that a lender's advertised rate may not apply if the amount of the loan request exceeds limits set by certain mortgage programs such as the Federal National Mortgage Association (Fannie Mae), FHA, VA, and the Federal Home Loan Mortgage Corporation (Freddie Mac). For example, at this time Fannie Mae and Freddie Mac criteria limit loans to $227,150 for a single-family residence. This limit may be adjusted upward from time to time.

Author's Notes

 Loan terms and rates change periodically. Be sure to check with a lender of your choice for the most up-to-date terms and conditions when you are in the market to purchase or refinance a property.

Keeping the Records Straight

by Valerie Terry, Director of Tax & Software

Jackson Hewitt, with over 2,000 offices nationwide, is the second largest tax preparation service in the United States. Michael Trainor, is Jackson Hewitt's president and CEO. Jackson Hewitt offers affordable and consistently high quality services, such as computerized tax preparation, electronic filing, refund anticipation loans, and accelerated check refunds. For more information, call 1-800-234-1040, visit their web site at http://www.jtax.com, or write to: Jackson Hewitt Tax Service, Attn: Tax & Software Department, 4575 Bonney Road, Virginia Beach, VA 23462-3831.

A vacation home is a home that is not your main home. It may be a house, co-op apartment, condominium, mobile home, boat, or similar property which has basic living accommodations, such as a sleeping space, a toilet, and cooking facilities. It does not include property used exclusively as a hotel, motel, inn, or similar establishment. A vacation home can also be your second home.

Personal Use vs. Rental Use of Your Vacation Property

When determining deductibility of expenses for your vacation property, you must divide your expenses between personal use and rental use. First, you must determine what is personal use and what is rental use.

You have personal use of your vacation property if you use it as your home. You use it as your home if you use it for personal purposes more than the greater of 14 days or 10% of the total days it is rented to others at a fair rental price. You can generally determine a fair rental price for your vacation property by using an amount that a person who is not related to you would be willing to pay. The rent is not a fair rental price if it is substantially lower than rents charged for other similar properties. Use the following criteria to determine if another property is similar to your property:

- The property is used for the same purpose.
- It is approximately the same size.
- It is in approximately the same condition.
- It has similar furnishings.
- It is in a similar location.

If the other property does not meet all of these criteria, it is probably not similar to yours.

Your vacation property is used for personal purposes any day it is used by you, by anyone else who has an interest in it, by your family members or by family members of those who have an interest in it (including siblings, half-siblings, spouses, parents, grandparents, children, grandchildren, etc.), by anyone under an arrangement that lets you use some other dwelling unit in exchange, or by anyone who uses it at less than a fair rental price.

Any days you spend at your vacation property working substantially full time repairing and maintaining your property are not counted as days of personal use even if family members use the property on the same days for recreational purposes. If you donate the use of your vacation property, it is considered to be used for personal purposes during that time. For example, if you donate the use of your vacation property to a charitable organization, and the organization sells the use of the property at a fund-raising event, the days the property is used by the purchaser are personal use days, not rental. Also, keep in mind that there is no deduction, charitable or otherwise, that can be taken as a result of donating use of your property for charitable purposes.

I'm proud of paying taxes. The only thing is – I could be just as proud for half the money.
— Arthur Godfrey

If during the year you only use your vacation property for personal purposes and do not rent it out, you will not have rental income or expenses. You can take allowable expenses as itemized deductions (explained later). If you use it for personal purposes and rent it less than 15 days, you do not include any of the rental income in your gross income, and you cannot deduct any of the expenses as rental expenses. You can still take allowable itemized deductions.

If during the year you do not use your vacation property for personal purposes at any time, you should report all rental income and deduct all rental expenses. If you use your vacation property as your home and rent it for 15 days or more, you have rental income and expenses. You must report all your rental income. If the income exceeds the rental expenses, including depreciation, deduct all rental expenses. If the rental income is less than the expenses, your deduction for expenses may be limited (discussed later).

Your vacation property is used for rental purposes any day it is rented at a fair rental price. Do not count days it is held out for rent but not actually rented. If you use your vacation property for personal and rental purposes, you must divide your expenses between the personal and rental use based on the number of days used for each purpose. To figure out the amount of rental expenses that can be deducted against the rental income, use the following formula:

$$\frac{\text{number of days used for rental}}{\text{total days used (rental + personal days)}}$$

Let's use as an example a vacation property that is used for personal purposes for 20 days out of the year and rented at fair rental value for 80 days.

$$80/(80 + 20) = 80/100 = 80\% \text{ rental use}$$

Rental expenses would be 80% of the total expenses.

Reporting Rental Income and Expenses

Rental income and expenses are reported on Schedule E, Supplemental Income and Loss (from rental real estate). Certain expenses incurred during non-rental periods for your vacation property can be taken on Schedule A, Itemized Deductions.

Rental Income

Rental income includes all amounts you receive for the use of your vacation property. If you receive property or services instead of money, your rental income would include the fair market value of the property or services. For example, if you trade a week's rental of your property for a set of golf clubs, the fair market value of the golf clubs would be considered rental income.

Allowable Expenses

Deductible expenses associated with a vacation property are divided into two major categories.

(1) Expenses incurred whether using the vacation property for personal or rental purposes must be prorated based upon the percentage of rental use. These expenses include home mortgage interest, real estate taxes, and casualty and theft losses. The rental portion of these expenses would be reported on Schedule E, and the remainder would be deducted as itemized deductions on Schedule A. If your vacation home is not used for rental purposes during the year (or is rented less than 15 days), deduct the full amount of mortgage interest, real estate taxes, and casualty and theft losses on Schedule A.

Exception: Mortgage interest. If you already own a first and second home, the portion of the mortgage interest for your vacation home (third home) not attributable as rental expenses is considered personal interest and is, therefore, not deductible.

Tip: If the deduction for rental expenses is limited (as discussed later), you can take out an equity loan on your main personal residence and use the money to pay off the debt on your vacation home. Generally, the loan interest will be fully deductible on Schedule A. Since you will no longer be taking a mortgage interest deduction for your vacation property, more of your other expenses will be allowable.

(2) Expenses associated strictly with the rental use of the property are 100% deductible. Some examples of these expenses are rental agency fees and advertising.

Some expenses can fall into both of these categories depending on the circumstances, such as repairs, maintenance, and utilities. For example, you may take your total yearly cost for utilities and multiply it by the percentage of rental use, or you may use 100% of the specific cost for utilities incurred only during the time the property was rented.

Repairs and Improvements. The rental percentage of expenses associated with repairing and maintaining your rental vacation home are deductible as rental expenses. If you make the repairs yourself, you can deduct the cost of materials used for the repairs but not the value of your time.

The cost of repairs is deductible but the cost of improvements is not. Repairs do not materially add to the value of property but keep your property in good operating condition. They include things like repainting, fixing leaks and floors, and replacing broken windows. Improvements add to the value of property, lengthen its useful life, or make it suitable for new uses. Some examples of improvements are room additions, landscaping, and installing a new roof, central heat and air conditioning, wall-to-wall carpeting, or a security system. Improvements can be depreciated (discussed later). If repairs are made as part of extensive remodeling or restoration, the whole job is an improvement.

Travel Expenses. Travel expenses that are ordinary and necessary costs of traveling to collect rental income are deductible. You can also deduct the rental portion of travel expenses associated with traveling to manage or maintain your rental vacation property. The standard mileage rate for tax year 1998 is 32.5 cents per mile. You may use the standard mileage rate to figure your deductible travel expenses for your vehicle, or you may use actual auto expenses.

Depreciation. Another expense associated with the rental of your vacation property is depreciation. Depreciation allows you to recover some or all of the cost of items used for rental purposes. The amount of depreciation that can be taken is mainly determined by four factors: (1) your basis in the property (generally its cost), (2) the recovery period for the property (or the number of years over which you can recover the basis of your property), (3) the date the property is placed in service (or when you started using it for rental purposes), and (4) the depreciation method and convention used. You can depreciate the rental percentage of property. Some commonly depreciable items for a rental vacation property are the house itself (not including the land value), furniture, and appliances. The basis for depreciable property is reduced by the amount of depreciation when figuring a gain or loss on its sale. If you are entitled to take depreciation but do not take it, the property's basis must still be reduced by the amount of depreciation that you should have deducted; so you should deduct the correct amount of depreciation each year.

Deduction Limits

As mentioned earlier, deductions for rental expenses may be limited if you use your vacation property as your home and rent it for 15 days or more. Generally, the rental expenses are limited to the amount of rental income. The rental portion of mortgage interest, real estate taxes, and casualty and theft losses, as well as expenses directly related only to the rental activity (such as rental agency fees, advertising, office supplies, postage, and commissions and fees) are fully deductible even if they exceed rental income. Other expenses are not deductible if the before-mentioned expenses created a rental loss; these other expenses are only deductible to the extent that the total of these and the fully deductible expenses do not exceed rental income. The other expenses include operating expenses (such as repairs, insurance, utilities, pest control, and lawn care) and depreciation. First, take the fully deductible expenses, then the operating expenses, and then depreciation. Any operating expenses and depreciation that you are not allowed to deduct in one year can be carried forward to the next year as rental expenses for the same vacation property. The same limits will apply the next year even if you do not use the property for personal purposes that year.

Record Keeping

You should keep records of all expenses associated with your vacation property. Since you should get a statement for the mortgage interest and real estate taxes paid, you do not have to keep separate records for those expenses, but you should keep separate records for all other expenses. Bills and statements related to your vacation property should be categorized by type to enable ready access to them.

Other Considerations

Condominium Dues or Assessments. If own a condominium as your vacation property, you also own part of the common elements of the entire building, such as lobbies and elevators, and you probably pay dues or assessments to take care of these elements. If you rent your condo, you can deduct the rental percentage of these dues or assessments. You cannot deduct special assessments paid to a condo management corporation for improvements, but you may be able to recover your share of the cost of improvements by taking depreciation.

Co-ops. If you have a cooperative apartment that you rent, you can usually deduct the rental percentage of the maintenance fees you pay the cooperative housing corporation. Any payments earmarked for a capital asset or improvement, or charged to the co-op's capital account cannot be deducted but must be added to the basis of your stock in the corporation. Deductibility of your portion of the co-op's mortgage interest and real estate taxes is figured the same as for any vacation property (discussed earlier). Your portion of interest and taxes is determined by dividing the number of shares of stock you own by the total outstanding shares and multiplying that amount by the co-op's total deductible interest and taxes. Typically, the co-op will figure the amount and send you a year-end statement.

Beside being able to deduct the rental percentage of your payments for repairs and upkeep for your co-op apartment, you can also deduct the rental portion of interest paid on a loan used to buy your stock in the co-op. You can also deduct your share of the co-op's depreciation.

Timeshares. Timeshares may be leased or owned depending on the terms of the purchase. Any interest on leased timeshares is considered personal interest, not mortgage interest, and is not deductible.

When You Sell

If you sell your vacation property, you will generally have a capital gain or loss. There may be other forms that will have to be filed, but the sale will ultimately be reported on Schedule D, Capital Gains and Losses. When figuring this gain or loss, the basis of the property must be reduced by the amount of depreciation (discussed earlier). You will need to use the capital gains tax rates to figure the tax on any gain from the sale. The Taxpayer Relief Act of 1997 generally reduces the tax on any net capital gain for sales (1) after May 6, 1997, and before July 29, 1997, for property held more than one year and (2) after July 28, 1997, for property held more than 18 months. The portion of the gain that relates to previous depreciation deductions is not eligible for the 10% and 20% capital gain tax rates. A 25% rate applies to gains realized after July 28, 1997, and held for more than 18 months.

Author's Notes

Tax regulations and laws change on a regular basis. Before buying or selling real property, be sure to obtain advice from your own tax or legal advisors for the most current laws and regulations.

This article and its contents are intended for general information only and should not be construed as legal or tax advice or a legal or tax opinion on specific facts and circumstances. They are not intended to be a substitute for obtaining legal advice from your own legal counsel or certified public accountant. Laws and regulations will change over time and should be interpreted only in light of particular circumstances

Resort Timesharing and Exchange:

Your Ticket to Vacation Variety

by Steve Miller

Steve Miller is the chief executive officer of Resort Condominiums International, LLC (RCI), a subsidiary of Cendant Corporation. Miller also serves as RCI's representative on the World Travel and Tourism Council (WTTC) and is a member of the American Resort Development Association (ARDA) Board of Directors and Executive Committee. He was named ARDA Leader of the Year in 1998.

RCI – the market leader in timeshare exchange service – has confirmed more than 13 million vacation exchanges since 1975. For more information, call (317) 876-1692, visit their web site at http://www.rci.com, or write to: RCI World Headquarters, 3502 Woodview Trace, Indianapolis, IN 46268-1104.

Vacations! What could be more inviting? A panoramic ocean view. A snow-covered mountain villa with a big fireplace. The heart of an exciting, bustling city with terrific shopping, dining, and entertainment. What's important to you when you think of taking a vacation? Going to a place that matches your interests and lifestyle? Variety and quality in your choice of location? Flexibility in the time of year you take your vacation? All of these elements are offered in one of today's alternative leisure concepts: resort timesharing, also known as vacation ownership.

Opportunities multiply as they are seized.
— Sun Tzu

Vacation ownership is a concept being considered by many. It has been identified by the World Tourism Organization as the fastest growing sector of the travel and leisure industry. Impressive growth statistics and the endorsement of leading hotel brands such as Hilton, Westin, and Ramada support this claim and reflect vacation ownership's rise in respectability:

- in 1980, worldwide vacation ownership sales were less than $500 million.
- in 1997, vacation ownership sales hit $6 billion.
- in 1990, 1.8 million people were timeshare owners. Today, there are nearly 4 million owners from more than 200 countries. They own at nearly 4,500 resort properties.
- owner satisfaction with vacation ownership is higher than 80%.

Traditional Timesharing

The timesharing concept originated in Europe in 1964. The concept was introduced to the United States in the early 1970s. Traditionally, timesharing was simple to define. It involved buying a part of a vacation property – a two-bedroom resort condominium at a beach property, for example – for only the period of time the owner planned to use it each year – two weeks at Christmas or one week in July.

Timesharing made sense for those vacationers who wanted home-like accommodations and more amenities – but didn't want to or couldn't afford to own a second home. Timesharing allowed them to own just the slice they needed – whether a week or two or six. With vacation costs controlled, plus comforts and amenities far beyond what the typical hotel offered, timeshare owners discovered a great vacation value.

Growth in Popularity

As today's vacation consumers demand added value and increased flexibility, vacation ownership promises to fulfill their expectations well into the future. According to *Hotel & Motel Management* magazine, the timeshare industry is expanding at approximately five times the rate of the traditional hospitality industry.

What makes timesharing so successful? Why is vacation ownership so popular that major hotel chains have been climbing aboard the timeshare bandwagon since the 1980s? Hilton, Ramada, Westin, and Sun International are all examples of hotel brands that have entered this arena. These companies see timesharing as a logical way to expand their product lines. Every major hotel brand is either offering a timeshare option today, or looking into it for the future.

The primary catalyst for the growth of the industry was the entry of the first vacation exchange service, Resort Condominiums International (RCI) in 1974. Vacation exchange was invented in response to the question often asked by consumers: "What if I don't want to vacation at the same place or the same time each year?"

Through RCI membership, timeshare owners can trade a week of ownership for a week in comparable resort accommodations in another state – or even another country. Vacation exchange jump-started the industry and, through the years, vacation exchange has continued to be singled out as the primary motivation for purchasing vacation ownership.

Geographic Expansion

While the hotel brands have become a prominent part of the timeshare landscape, the industry continues to be comprised primarily of independent developers and operators. One of the first recognized groups to embrace the timeshare industry was Fairfield Communities, which is also in the community development business. Today, Fairfield is one of the top names in timesharing, with 19 resorts and 160,000 timeshare owners.

Vistana Resort, which debuted in Orlando in 1981, is considered to be the model for a successful single-site development. Vistana went public in 1997 and is now expanding through joint ventures with Promus Hotels and the PGA of America.

Today's fastest growing timeshare developer/operator is Signature Resorts, with 81 properties and more than 200,000 owners.

As timesharing has developed into a viable vacation option, the major players in the hospitality industry have joined the business. Hilton Hotels rolled out with the Hilton Grand Vacations Club in 1993. Embassy Vacation Resorts raised its timeshare flag in 1994. Following shortly on its heels was the launch of Ramada Vacation Suites in 1995. Most recently, Westin Hotels & Resorts has introduced a timeshare product.

More Flexible Purchase Options

In addition to geographic expansion, the industry has become more responsive to consumer demands for greater flexibility. Biennial time-shares now allow vacationers to purchase vacation time for use every other year. The split-use option gives owners the ability to divide their

Crossroad Ahead!

There are many roads that could lead to your vacation property dream. Look both ways at each road that crosses the main highway before making your final decision.

Interested in taking a look at timesharing, my wife and I recently spent the better part of a Saturday afternoon touring a Fairfield Communities time-share resort near Orlando. The sales agent was both pleasant and professional. At the end of his presentation, he and his manager explained that, even within the world of timesharing, several purchase options are available.

The first option, if we bought that afternoon, was a week of timesharing for $15,000, a price that was sure to go up in the next month or two. That week could be used at the Fairfield Communities Orlando resort or traded through the Fairfield Communities network of resorts or through Resort Condominiums International (RCI) for vacations at other resorts. Also, they explained, we would receive a valuable package of initial visit incentive gifts. For example, they would pay our annual membership to RCI for the first 3 years.

As an alternative, the manager then offered us the "every other year program." This costs half of the regular plan and can be used every other year. The manager explained that once we bought this plan, we could always upgrade it to the regular yearly program, if we desired.

Finally, the exit interviewer offered us one more option. For about $800, we could purchase a one-week vacation package at a Fairfield resort. As he explained it, this would give us a chance to try out the program without making a long term commitment.

TIP Although we decided not to buy at this time, the tour gave us the chance to see a very nice resort and learn about the timeshare concept and the various purchase options available. Not only that, we received a $50 restaurant gift certificate as well as a certificate for a 2-night, 3-day stay at our choice of other Fairfield Communities timeshare resorts.

time into two shorter getaways. Timeshare properties continue to offer new and more flexible options for owners – even allowing for use of their vacation time in one-day increments.

Many resorts now offer points-based reservation systems, which give owners the flexibility to use their vacations in a variety of ways. Under some timeshare plans, points can even be redeemed for products and services other than accommodations – including cruises, airline tickets, and tours.

Stress-Free Vacationing

Americans insist they need less stress and more vacations. Results from the YP&B/Yankelovich Partners 1998 National Leisure Travel MONITOR study show greater work demands, more complexity, and a time shortage combine to create greater anxiety in Americans' lives and an even greater need to escape. And wherever they are escaping to, vacationers want the planning phase to be stress-free. Planning a timeshare vacation opens up a world of opportunities that timeshare owners might never have otherwise had the chance to experience.

Stress-free – but new and different, too. Today's vacationers aren't willing to give up excitement and new adventures. There's enthusiasm for sampling new cuisine, cruising, visiting theme parks, learning new skills or activities, gaming, and eco-vacations.

Variety, yes – complexity, no. As part of that philosophy, consumers want their vacation accommodations to be convenient – a home away from home. Such accommodations allow vacationers to kick back comfortably at the end of an action-filled day, perhaps to fix a quick meal in the kitchen, throw a load of beach towels and swimsuits in the washer, watch a box office hit on the video player – or even sink into a soothing whirlpool tub. While amenities vary among resort properties, almost all offer separate bedrooms, full kitchen, and appealing decor.

What the Future Holds

In the years ahead, the number of timeshare-owner families in the United States is expected to increase at least ten-fold. About one-third of U.S. households qualified to purchase timesharing, on the basis of annual income and interest in the timeshare experience, will actually become owners. That number is up from about 4 percent in 1995.

Consider these statistics, provided by RCI and the American Resort Development Association (ARDA):

- 75% of timeshare owners would recommend timesharing to people they know.
- 41% of timeshare owners own more than one interval (week).
- 23% of timeshare owners are interested in purchasing additional vacation time.
- 73% of timeshare owners say they've enjoyed vacations more since they've become owners.
- 67% of timeshare owners say their lives have been positively impacted just by being a timeshare owner.

Vacation Exchange Services

RCI – the market leader – does not own, but has contracts with more than 3,300 timeshare resorts in almost 90 countries, and booked more than 1.8 million exchanges in 1997, sending some 6.5 million people on vacation. RCI's more than 2.3 million member families (timeshare owners) reside in more than 200 countries. Seven out of every 10 timeshare resorts worldwide are affiliated with RCI and eight out of every 10 vacation exchanges are fulfilled through RCI. Since 1975, RCI has confirmed more than 13 million vacation exchanges.

In a snapshot view, here's how timesharing works. For a one-time purchase price and an annual maintenance fee, timeshare purchasers own their vacation location forever, or for a predetermined number of years, depending upon the purchase agreement. Often, people discover time-share opportunities while they are on a vacation. They find that they enjoy the area and facility so much, that a timeshare purchase makes sense.

Timesharing is not a financial investment, but it is considered a lifestyle investment. Timesharing eliminates the hassles of upkeep and the worry of renting the condominium. By virtue of being a timeshare owner and an RCI member, the consumer has a multitude of vacation options for years to come. According to the MONITOR study, 54% of respondents intend to vacation at a condominium resort within the next two years. Seventeen percent of leisure travelers say they have an interest in purchasing a resort timeshare.

Adding greatly to the satisfaction level of timesharing is the vacation exchange option. The RCI exchange process is simple. If a member wants to exchange the vacation time they own for another location, he or she simply deposits that time in a special pool of inventory. The pool is like a bank in which the vacation time that RCI members deposit creates the reserves from which RCI transacts the exchanges. Once the deposit has been made and the member has determined where they want to travel, they can request comparable accommodations from the RCI inventory pool in return.

RCI, which employs nearly 4,000 vacation industry professionals in 40 offices in 30 countries, is headquartered in Indianapolis, Indiana. It is owned by Cendant Corporation which is the world's leading consumer- and business-services organization. Cendant operates in three principal segments: membership services, travel and real estate. RCI is part of the travel services group, along with leading brands such as Days Inn®, Howard Johnson®, Ramada® and Avis®. Cendant real estate brands include Coldwell Banker®. Cendant services some 70 million member-ships and makes more than 100 million consumer contacts each year.

RCI operates a closed membership program, with most benefits available only to RCI members and affiliated resorts. The general consumer can explore timesharing opportunities through a national condominium rental program called Extra Holidays, which is operated by RCI.

RCI's Web site – www.rci.com – provides a wealth of information about timesharing, vacation exchange and RCI.

Conclusion

Opportunities. That's what timesharing and vacation exchange are all about. This increasingly popular way to vacation provides variety, flexibility, and quality choices for your leisure time and dollars. Vacation exchange programs like that of RCI offer millions of consumers a way to vacation that ensures them opportunities to see the world – and own a small corner of it at the same time.

This article is for informational purposes only. Readers are advised to consult with their own accountants/financial consultants prior to purchasing a timeshare interval.

Interior Design Tips for Rental Property Owners

by Kenneth D. Ratcliffe

Ken Ratcliffe is president of Seltar Interiors, an Orlando area company he founded in 1987. A graduate of the University of Florida, Ken and Seltar's American Society of Interior Designers (ASID) team have rendered their expertise for clients, including timeshares, resorts, and developers throughout the U.S. and the Caribbean. For more information, call (407) 365-5292 or write to: Seltar Interiors, 209 South Central Avenue, Oviedo, FL 32765.

Whether furnishing a new vacation property, or refurbishing an existing one, the following suggestions will help ensure that you receive maximum value for the dollars you spend. If you only remember one thing from reading this chapter, remember this: there are major differences between rental property furnishings and residential furnishings. You don't believe me? Read on.

When considering interior furnishings, select items specifically designed for use in a rental environment. The furnishings in your rental property will sustain wear and tear on a much greater scale than your home furnishings. Like it or not, people simply will not take care of your rental property the way you do. It's just human nature.

You must also remind yourself that your rental property is not your home. You must be willing to repress personal taste a bit, in favor of what best meets the needs of your investment. Ask yourself three basic questions concerning the furnishings in your rental property: 1) are they appealing; 2) are they comfortable; and, 3) will they last.

While you are likely to select your home furnishings based primarily on personal likes and dislikes, your rental property furnishing selections must include appeal, practicality, and durability as part of the decision. Your rental property will be subjected to sand, suntan oil, snow, mud, dropped food, parties, and spilled drinks (grape Kool-Aid is my personal favorite), just to name a few. Windows and doors will be left open, wet towels will be tossed on beds, ice-filled glasses will sit for hours on tables. Do you know the proper furnishings needed to survive this carnage?

One last thought before we move on. Consider carefully where you purchase your rental property furnishings. As noted above, there are definite and critical differences between residential and rental property furnishings, and not every salesperson knows, cares, or has the experience, to guide you in the right direction. For a variety of reasons, many will sell you the wrong furnishings: they have too much stock of a particular item; their profit margin is higher on a certain item; they simply do not understand the different requirements of rental property furnishings; etc.

Whether you think you can or think you can't, you're right.
— Henry Ford

If possible, purchase from a company that has experience furnishing rental properties. Consult a professional interior designer in the field. Ask what properties they have furnished. Visit those properties yourself. Request references.

If you are like most people, it is very difficult for you to restrict your personal preferences. Consequently, your furnished rental property winds up reflecting too much of your personal taste, and not enough of what the property needs to be successful financially. An interior designer can steer you down the proper path, and avoid this common pitfall. They can point you towards the things that work, away from the things that won't, and in general, create a furnishings package that is fully coordinated.

They can provide you with the best furniture layout for your floor plan, as well as the best scale, style, and selection for your particular property. Obviously, not all areas, locales, or properties should be furnished the same. Properties often have distinct themes. People travel to specific areas for specific reasons, and they expect your unit to reflect that ambiance. A traveler to Florida's beaches would be most surprised to find a rental property furnished in dark woods and heavy fabrics. A rental property owner in the mountains would be ill advised to furnish their

Caution: Road Forks Ahead!

Once you have purchased your vacation property, one of your first priorities will be to furnish the unit with furniture, household goods, and window treatments. Will you do it yourself or work with an interior planning and design firm?

After we bought a one-bedroom condo, we opted to furnish it ourselves. We relied on our taste and good judgment to select the furnishings. Thinking we could save money, we found a large furniture store in Charleston and spent several days choosing all of the items: queen-size bed, frame, and headboard, artwork, lamps, end tables, dressers, kitchenware, dining room table, glass top table and chairs for the porch, sleeper sofa, color television with stand, and other items required by our rental management company to rent our condo through their rental pool.

Did we take the right fork in the road? Looking back on it now, I don't believe so!

Cost savings? Maybe we saved a little money. Maybe not. Most design firms make their profit from the wholesale discounts they receive from the furniture manufacturers. Some charge an hourly fee for their planning and design in addition to the itemized furniture costs.

Quality furnishings? We did not know at the time about industrial strength spring mechanisms for the sleeper sofa. Nor did we understand that a commercial grade carpeting would hold up better under the increased wear of a vacation condo. A good interior designer would know these furnishing techniques. Also, the designer would provide a unified, coordinated "look and feel" to the condo.

Time savings? I know we spent a lot of time furnishing the condo ourselves. We spent days, even weeks on this project, which could have been better spent enjoying our vacation home.

TIP When evaluating the pros and cons of furnishing your vacation property yourself, be sure to consider all of the professional services that may be rendered by an interior designer. Calculate and compare savings in both time and money before making your choice. In the long haul, I think you'll find it to your advantage to put the professionals to work for you.

property in pastels and rattan. If I've just described your rental property, you should know now why you never seem to get any rentals. Call a professional quickly!!

Professionals are able to access many more sources than you can, and they get much better pricing. They aren't just purchasing for you, they are purchasing for many different people, and oftentimes get considerable price breaks from the manufacturers. In fact, many designers buy direct from the manufacturers, eliminating the middle man and producing even greater savings.

Don't think you have to give up total control to use a designer. Most will welcome and encourage your input and ideas, and help you establish realistic budget parameters. If you're like most buyers, you bought your rental property to provide yourself an occasional getaway, hoping to keep it rented as much as possible to help offset expenses. Using an experienced professional to help maximize the interior impact is a logical step towards achieving that goal.

All this may sound like a bit of extra effort, but remember: it's increased money in your pocket if your property is rented more, and refurbished less.

Now let's consider some specifics.

Flooring

Bear in mind that there is a great deal of flooring in your unit, and it takes a tremendous amount of wear. Due to quantity alone, flooring will have a major impact on the look of your unit, and will be among the more expensive items to replace. Choose flooring that is both attractive and durable.

In carpeted areas, avoid light colors that will easily show traffic paths and stains. In the industry, there is a saying that most carpets don't wear out, they "ugly out." Think about carpets with deeper color values and/or small patterns, both of which are excellent at concealing wear and stains. Choose carpets that are bright and cheery. Also, if the carpet is over pad, make sure that the pad is of good quality as well. A substandard carpet pad will hasten the breakdown of the carpet and in some cases can void the manufacturer's warranty.

There are many different carpets available in both commercial and residential types. Commercial carpet usually has a tighter weave and lower pile. This results in a fade resistant carpet that does not allow soil or sand into the pile. Commercial carpet will last for a longer time, but may not retain its look. Regarding colors and patterns, there is usually less of a selection in commercial carpets that is appropriate for rental property.

Residential carpet is usually plusher and has a higher pile. You will have much more of a selection of both colors and styles in residential carpet, but because of its higher pile, residential carpet is not as forgiving of traffic patterns.

Whatever type carpet you choose, keep in mind they are both made with two basic types of yarn: nylon and olefin. Nylon has the longer track record, having been used in the carpet industry for many years. Nylon yarns have changed over the years, and the most current is "solution dyed" nylon, which provides more resistance to cleaning chemicals, and fading. Nylon, customarily speaking, wears better, but it also costs more.

Olefin yarns are more resistant than nylon yarns to cleaning chemicals and fading, but they can have a quicker tendency to pack down and show traffic patterns. In general, olefin based carpets are less expensive than their solution dyed nylon counterparts.

When buying carpet, do not use the ounce weight of the carpet as your sole criteria. Other factors to consider are pile height, stitches per inch, and gauge. Also inquire about the type of stain resistance treatments and warranties provided by the manufacturer, and have your carpet installed by a reputable installer.

Ceramic Tile

Consider using ceramic tile or vinyl in entryways and areas where food will usually be present. These areas are among the first and worst to show wear, stains, etc. While vinyl is less expensive than tile, tile makes a much more impressive statement, particularly as a first impression upon entering the foyer. If utilized in small areas, tile can add a great deal of impact for the cost involved, and is very durable. Make certain to use only non-skid tiles, and opt for larger size tiles. Use 12 X 12 tiles, or if your room is big enough, even 16 X 16.

The color of your floor tile grout is also important. Grout by nature is very porous. Light colored grout will quickly turn dark as it absorbs particles from the water used in daily cleaning. Use a medium to deep color grout. It will retain it's color and resist taking on the dark, dirty appearance to which light colored grout is so susceptible.

A note of caution. Avoid using too many different floorings in close proximity. Tile in the foyer next to vinyl in the kitchen next to carpet in the living room, tends to make your rental property appear chopped up and smaller. Try to use no more than two different flooring materials within the same visible area.

Upholstered Items

Many of the same principles apply to upholstered furnishings as to carpet. Select fabrics that are attractive, but more importantly, they need to wear well and hide soiling. Avoid light colors and polished cottons, instead steering towards heavier grade, patterned fabrics. The latest advance in fabrics are all-weather fabrics, originally designed for outdoor use, but now making their way inside. These fabrics are 100% acrylic or polyester, very resistant to stains and fading, and available in an increasing assortment of colors and patterns. You can even scrub them with a light brush!

Many people ask about stain-guard treatments for fabrics. Be very careful here. Treatment applied by anyone other than the manufacturer can drastically alter the colors in many fabrics, and also may void the manufacturer's warranty on the fabric. Make sure you investigate these concerns before you act.

Once you have selected your fabrics, you're now ready to choose the pieces to put your fabrics on. When choosing a sofa style, consider whether the back cushions are loose or attached. Loose cushions have a tendency to be taken off and used as floor cushions, etc., in a rental situation. Also, select wooden arms or use arm covers on upholstered arms.

Sleeper Sofa

There is no better example of the difference between residential and rental use than a sleeper sofa. A sleeper sofa in a residence gets used very infrequently (assuming no one is in the doghouse). But in a rental property, the sleeper sofa will be utilized almost daily. For this reason, the sleeper mechanism must be able to withstand the wear of regular use, and the mattress should be comfortable. A commercial sleeper mechanism and a reversible innerspring mattress are musts. The commercial mechanism will withstand the extensive use (kids like sleeper sofas as trampolines), and the reversible mattress will last longer, and give you a better night's sleep. Make certain that the mattress is rotated and turned on a regular basis for maximum life-span.

While fully upholstered chairs are often used in some areas of your rental property, dining chairs should not be fully upholstered. You should choose dining chairs with upholstered seats only, or at most upholstered seats and backs. Food and drink are the biggest enemies of dining chairs and barstools, so thought should be given to appropriate fabric protection. Utilizing vinyl, or laminating the seat fabric prevents soiling and extends greatly the life of the chair.

When the seat fabric does become soiled, or you decide to change your decor, simply have the seats (and backs) reupholstered. This is much less expensive than replacing the entire chair. Dining chairs and barstools should be armless unless you have plenty of room in your dining area. Always keep in mind the scale of the room you are attempting to furnish, and choose accordingly. Large, high-back chairs can shrink a room immensely, and reduce smooth traffic flow through your unit.

Wallpaper

The best advice to keep in mind regarding wallpaper is to use it sparingly. Mildew is a problem, especially in tropical or waterfront properties, and in any other location where moisture is a factor. Wallpaper does not allow the walls to breathe, thus the moisture builds between the wallpaper and the drywall, forming that lovely purple mildew and that wonderful musty smell. Another problem with wallpaper is that it can be expensive to replace when you want to change your decor, especially if there is mildew damage to the drywall.

Instead, consider wallpapering just the baths and kitchen. These are typically small areas and can be less expensively replaced. Use paint and wallpaper borders in other areas you wish to treat. Paint is very easy to change, and moisture is not a problem with wallpaper borders. And don't just put all borders at ceiling height. Think about putting the borders at chair-rail height; drop them down 6-8 inches from the ceiling; etc. Vary the placement of the wallpaper borders to create a different look and feel for different rooms.

Case Goods

Case goods are your tables, nightstands, dressers, etc., and making the correct choice here can greatly reduce how often these pieces have to be replaced. For obvious reasons, case good pieces do not generally have to be replaced as often as upholstered goods. If you buy wisely, that is. The major component all case goods in your rental property should have, is a laminated or glass top. This prevents "rings" when iced drinks are left unattended, and resists scratches as well.

There are advantages and disadvantages to glass. It can break, creating a safety (and liability) hazard. It is difficult to keep clean, particularly in waterfront properties where the nice moist breeze coats everything. And it is easily scratched. On the positive side, glass creates a very light, bright, open look for your property, and visually makes your rooms look bigger. If you decide to use glass, it should be inset, of the proper thickness, and have no sharp edges or corners.

Laminate is a very durable surface that is extremely resistant to water, stains, and scratches. You can choose from a variety of colors and styles. Laminate also has a bright, light appearance, and is easier to keep clean than glass. Either surface will work well for you, keeping your furnishings looking new for years. Keep in mind that utilizing both glass and laminate tops (mix and match) within your rental property is a great idea. Varying the surfaces creates the more relaxed, less formal look that people on vacation are looking for.

In your living room, bear in mind that there will often be someone sleeping on the sleeper sofa. Those persons need clothing storage, and to utilize the sleeper, they should be able to move the cocktail table easily. If the cocktail table is awkward to move, it may get damaged as people struggle with it. You can accommodate the clothing storage need with a television armoire in your living room. Consider something with a couple of drawers underneath where the television sits.

You should also ensure that any case goods you purchase have metal side guides on all drawers, and not wooden guides. The wooden guides swell from moisture, and then the drawers fail to open properly. Of course people then damage the drawers trying to get them open and closed. Insist on metal guides!! Also, if possible, stay away from any brass trim on your case good purchases, especially around waterfront properties. Brass tends to pit and rust.

Beds

If you want to create a certain source of complaints, put inferior bedding in your rental property. Since people spend eight hours a day in bed, it makes obvious sense that you choose bedding that is comfortable. In the master bedroom, use as large a bed as possible without overwhelming the room, or restricting normal movement in the room.

Deciding what size beds to put in secondary bedrooms depends on who you anticipate using your unit. If your property attracts a lot of families, then twin beds might be appropriate. If your renters tend to be mostly adults or couples traveling together, utilize the same advice noted earlier for master bedrooms.

Mattresses should be of reasonable quality, and have side support. Side support is a heavy gauge wire around the inside mattress edge. This prevents sagging and helps the mattress retain its shape longer. You should ensure that the mattress is rotated regularly and properly (end to end, and over), which will also add years to the life of the mattress. Under the mattress, we recommend box springs as opposed to a foundation. Box springs provide more constant support and comfort.

Your bedspread fabric should have the same qualities as upholstered items. Avoid light and solid colors, choosing instead patterned, deeper color values that are bright and cheery, but capable of hiding stains and soiling. We suggest using Trevira fabric for your bedspreads (Trevira may not be available through all retail sources, but is readily available through design sources). Trevira is inherently flame retardant, resistant to fading, and machine washable. Bedspreads should be quilted, and have a minimum of 5-6 ounces of fill for that plump, full appearance.

Window Treatments

The window treatments you select will depend on your budget. Obviously, you should ensure that whatever treatments you select provide complete privacy, as well as block out sunlight. This can be accomplished with fabric draperies, mini-blinds, or a combination of the two. We do not recommend vertical blinds. Verticals are a maintenance nightmare. People don't know how to use them properly, open doors and windows leave them blowing in the wind, the tracks break, vanes break, etc.

Blackout-lined, baton draw, fabric draperies cost a bit more initially, but they will last much longer, and have almost no maintenance problems. If you insist on purchasing verticals, at least get self-rotating tracks, which open and close the vanes automatically when the verticals are drawn.

The fabric you choose should again be Trevira, in colors that will hide soiling and dirt. For top treatments, consider at least the more important areas such as the living room, dining room, and master bedroom. A point to note here. It is much better to have your fabric treatments in a solid or companion fabric to your sofa or bedspread fabric, than to match them exactly. Why? If you want or need to replace the sofa or bed-spread, and that fabric is no longer available, you would then have to replace the window treatments as well. If the window treatments are in a companion fabric, they may be salvageable.

Miscellaneous

Lastly, there are a few miscellaneous thoughts on items you will purchase for your rental property. Televisions, for instance, where bigger is better. At the absolute minimum in the living room or main viewing area, select a 25" television. Preferably larger. And consider purchasing a commercial television. It will have many attractive features (volume limiting, AM-FM stereo radio, channel labeling, etc.), and it will be warranted for commercial use. Many rental property owners find out too late that the great bargain TV they purchased is not warranted for use in a rental property. Commercial televisions are very reasonably priced, and well worth it for the features you receive.

For other locations in your rental unit, again, bigger is better. A minimum 19" TV should go in the master and secondary bedrooms, and all televisions should be connected to cable. Other options include a VCP or VCR. A VCP will only play tapes, it does not record. The advantage of a VCP over a VCR is that there is less to break or go wrong, and most people on vacation don't particularly care about recording tapes, just viewing them.

Patio furniture should be sufficient for the number of persons in your rental unit (otherwise your living and dining room chairs wind up outside). Lamps should have three-way switches, and no brass bases (they will rust and pit). Artwork should not be framed in brass for the same reason. Artwork with washed wood frames and colorful matting adds a nice touch to your unit.

In your housewares package, beside the standards (coffee maker, toaster, etc.), consider a microwave, blender, and inexpensive plastic glasses (great for the pool or patio). Towels and sheets do not have to be top of the line, but towels should be ample size and weight, and sheets should be clean and in good shape.

Mirrored walls are a great way to make a small space appear larger or a dull space more exciting. Utilize mirrored bi-fold closet doors in the bedroom(s). Dining areas are often small, so a mirrored wall serves to expand the space. Remember that it is not always necessary to mirror from floor to ceiling. Mirroring a wall from ceiling to chair rail height can be very dramatic. Do try to have the mirror reflect something of interest and not a blank wall. Mirroring opposite a window is the ideal. If that is not possible or practical, mirror opposite a picture or other item of impact.

Summary

The best advice I can leave you with is to step back and take an objective look at your rental unit. The more appealing, comfortable, and enjoyable your unit is to stay in, the more likely renters are to return, and to recommend it to their friends. Following the tips in this article will help ensure you are doing all you can to maximize rental income, while minimizing furnishings cost.

Good luck and best wishes for years of enjoyment from your properly furnished and decorated vacation property!

AFTER YOU BUY

Put $$Thousands$$ of Extra Rental Revenue
In Your Pocket

Your Property Rental Manager Is Your Business Partner

You would have a most difficult time owning a vacation property at the seashore or on the ski slopes (and probably hundreds of miles from your primary residence) without having someone nearby or on-site to manage the property.

Considering their importance, you should definitely know your rental manager's name, just as you know your attorney's name and your accountant's name.

You shouldn't own a vacation property without a property manager. Your property manager wouldn't have a business without you and other owners. You are business partners.

Many owners don't realize the importance of their property manager. They don't take the time to understand the complexity and scope of the property manager's business. Therefore, some owners are not properly using this valuable human and business resource to get the most from their property investment.

The best executive is the one who has sense enough to pick good men to do what he wants done, and self-restraint enough to keep from meddling with them while they do it.
— Theodore Roosevelt

The key here is to foster better understanding between owners and property managers, eliminating distrust and building a solid business foundation that is mutually beneficial. How do you foster better understanding? Through better communication.

Communications can be as basic as a listing of services that the management company provides. Many owners don't realize the full extent of the services available from the management company. Better service for owners means more profit for property managers. Your management company may offer all or some of the following services:

- Rentals
- Property maintenance
- Cleaning/housekeeping
- Spring cleaning/deep cleaning
- Winterizing services
- Deliveries to the property
- Purchase and delivery of gifts to guests (flowers, fruit baskets, champagne, etc.)
- Bike rentals
- Information on area restaurants and activities
- Welcome kits with soaps, shampoo, and other personal items
- Provision of cribs and strollers
- Provision of cots and extra beds
- Distribution of keys to the property
- Accounting services (monthly and year-end)
- Replacement of heating and air conditioning filters (routinely)
- Inventory of furnishings
- Replacement of furnishings
- Carpet cleaning and replacement
- Advice and counsel on keeping the property in top rental shape
- Pre- and post-rental inspections
- Cleaning and security deposit distribution and disputes

The above list can serve as a guide or checklist when you interview property managers to hire for your vacation property.

Find out what services the management company offers, and take advantage of as many of them as you possibly can. The more tasks you can delegate to your business partner, the more time you will be able to devote to other things, like finding additional rentals or simply enjoying your property.

CAUTION: Double Curve!

How much does it take to change a light bulb? Imagine my dismay when I discovered on my monthly rental statement that it took $20 at my property at Kiawah Island!

Incredulous and slightly upset, I called my property manager and asked, "How in the world can you charge me $20 for a single light bulb?"

She checked my records and explained: "You had a burned out bulb in the designer lamp in your living room area. After we discovered the problem, we had to make a special trip to the hardware store in Charleston to get a similar bulb. In addition to the actual cost of the bulb, which was about $4, we charged you for a portion of the time and mileage of the trip to get the new bulb."

TIP *I thought about what she said. I knew which lamp it was. The bulb had lasted much longer than expected. And a 30 to 40 mile round trip to the hardware store would take well over an hour. Suddenly, $20 sounded pretty cheap. I thanked her for the information and for changing the burned out bulb.*

Had my rental manager included a full explanation of this charge on my statement, it would have saved me a lot of aggravation, it would have saved me from making a phone call, and it would have saved her the trouble of checking the records and explaining the charge to me.

If you wish, you can consult a local Coldwell Banker office for suggestions on property management services in the area of your interest (see the directory of Coldwell Banker Resort Property Network offices in Section 5 of this book).

Crisis Communication

As a vacation property owner, you must expect the unexpected. For example, Hurricane Hugo visited Kiawah Island in 1989. We were lucky. The Island escaped Hugo's direct hit, although a major effort was required to clean up fallen trees and debris following the hurricane. Before and after the disaster, our management company kept in contact with us. During the crisis, we were most appreciative of the daily updates from our management company.

Hurricanes, thunderstorms, snow storms, floods, lightning strikes and other tricks Mother Nature has up her sleeve can hit at any time. Our property was once struck by lightning. Our management company assessed the damage, assisted our guests who were in the property during the storm, and promptly called us with the news. We immediately called our guests and expressed our concern for their safety. We asked our management company to deliver a bottle of wine to our guests and a teddy bear to their daughter, who had been frightened by the storm.

You're only as good as the people you hire. — Ray Kroc

Our management company took care of all the necessary repairs, replacing the drapes and carpet and arranging for the interior painting. Within a week, they had the unit back in tip top shape and ready for our next visitors.

Positive Reinforcement

Communications are vital during a crisis. But it is also important for property owners to tell their rental manager when they are doing a great job.

Several seasons ago, we had two weeks in July that we thought would go unrented. I called our management company and informed them we had two prime weeks available and I would appreciate their help in putting some heads in beds in my villa. In the meantime, I tried to fill the weeks with some personal marketing – calls to friends, relatives, and business associates – all to no avail.

I thought I had lost two prime rental weeks until I got my July rental statement. Lo and behold! The rental management company had rented both weeks, so that my unit was fully booked for the month of July!

I will have no man work for me who has not the capacity to become a partner. — J.C. Penney

Two weeks of rentals I was not expecting translated into $1400 in revenue. I was delighted. I called my management company and asked the manager to buy some beer and wine for the staff. "Please have a mini happy hour on us after work today," I said, "and bill me for the champagne and beer on this month's rental statement."

Apparently, not many owners take the time and effort to compliment their rental managers. My gesture made quite an impression. Several weeks later when I called to check on some guests, I spoke to one of the reservationists.

CAUTION: Slippery When Wet!

The temptation is always to get involved in the cleaning and maintenance chores at your vacation property.

Often during our weeks at Kiawah Island, my wife Terry and I (but, to be honest, mostly Terry) got involved in cleaning and refurbishing our property. For example, on one "vacation" to our condo, we painted the porch floor. During another trip, we ordered a new sleeper sofa and made sure we were at the condo when it was delivered. On yet another vacation, we ordered new carpeting and supervised the installation.

On almost all of our vacations at our property, Terry and I spent a lot of time maintaining and cleaning the condo. The morning of our departure often found us still cleaning.

In retrospect, I believe we got too involved in the maintenance and upkeep of the property. Our rental management company could have done all of the cleaning and refurbishing that we elected to do ourselves. Granted, we may have saved a little money by doing this work ourselves. And Terry maintains (rightfully so, I'm afraid) that she does a much more thorough job of cleaning.

 Nevertheless, I recommend that property owners delegate this work to the rental management company.

Your vacations are supposed to provide recreation and relaxation – not maintenance hassles. Your last morning at your vacation property should be spent playing a round of golf or a few sets of tennis. Perhaps a long walk on the beach or two more runs down the slopes. You shouldn't spend your last precious moments dusting, vacuuming, doing laundry, or scouring sinks and tubs.

My advice is to let your rental management company maintain and clean your property. That is why they are there. You are there to enjoy your vacation.

"Oh, Mr. Cain," she said, "Thank you so much for the champagne. It is so nice to know that some of our owners appreciate the job we do for them. It was very considerate of you to buy us some wine. What a nice touch!"

When you go out of your way to thank your property manager, your property manager will continue to go out of his/her way to help you.

Action Steps:

 Know your rental manager's name and keep in constant communication with them.

 Avail yourself of the full range of services provided by your management company.

 Be sure to show your appreciation for a job well done.

Get Extra Rentals Yourself

You've purchased your place in the sun...a second home for vacations, an A-frame or chalet on the ski slopes, a condominium on the ocean, a cottage on the lake, a villa in the desert or a cabin in the mountains. You plan to enjoy the property yourself for two weeks of the year, and you've hired a management company to maintain the property and locate renters for the remainder of the year. Congratulations! You have achieved a dream shared by many.

The man who rolls up his sleeves seldom loses his shirt.
— Thomas Cowan

With a monthly mortgage payment of, let us say, $1200 and a weekly rental rate of $1000, you calculate that, even if the property is only rented two weeks out of the month, you will come out ahead, right?

Maybe. Maybe not. Remember that, in addition to your monthly mortgage payment, you will also pay for furnishings, property taxes, insurance, regime or commons charges, sewer and water, electricity, base telephone charges, repairs, maintenance, commissions, and management fees.

The single biggest opportunity you will have to ensure a positive cash flow is the occupancy rate of your property.

The following chapters in this section provide valuable marketing, advertising, and publicity information which can help you attract renters to your property.

A good management company is a valuable business partner. But don't think that, having hired them, you must rely on them completely to locate renters. You can supplement their efforts.

Evaluate Your Property

The first thing you should do is analyze your property. List all of its features and the attractions of the resort and the surrounding area. These highlights are really the reasons someone would want to buy your product... why someone would rent your property.

No doubt you analyzed the pluses and minuses of the property before you purchased it, so this step should be easy. Your list might look something like this:

Your Property
- Large, one-bedroom condominium
- Fully furnished, including queen-size bed, dishwasher, sheets and towels, glassware, dishes, washer and dryer, color TV, hide-a-bed sofa, etc.
- Central heat and air-conditioning
- Screened-in porch
- Kitchen/dining room
- Decorator-furnished
- On the ocean
- In the middle of the resort
- Bicycles included in rental price
- Olympic pool complex nearby

The Resort
- On the ocean with 10 miles of beach
- Golf on three championship courses
- 40 tennis courts in two complexes
- Warm, sunny climate
- Fishing, both fresh and salt water; ocean charter boats available for hire
- Wildlife refuge for safaris, sightseeing, photography
- Gourmet restaurants at the resort
- Shopping at the resort
- Supervised activities for children
- Special events – planned and promoted by the resort
- Excellent night life

The Area

- One hour from international airport
- 15 minutes from private airport
- Near major metropolitan area
- Interstate highways
- Excellent restaurants, shopping, cultural events

Of course, if you own a chalet on the ski slopes, or another type of resort property, the features of the resort and the area will be greatly different from those listed above. But, the features of the chalet, the condo, or the second home might be very similar.

> *I am a great believer in luck, and I find that the harder I work, the more I have of it.*
> — Thomas Jefferson

When you communicate these features to prospective renters, always tell them how they will benefit. The car salesman sells the tilt-steering wheel option by relating how it will benefit the car's owner: "The tilt-steering wheel makes it easier to get in and out of your car. It improves your driving comfort since you can adjust the wheel to your preferred level. And it increases the resale value of the car."

Tell your customers how they will benefit from the features of your property:

Feature: Fully furnished kitchen, including cookware, tableware, refrigerator, microwave, range, and dishwasher.

Benefit: Vacationers will save money by preparing and eating some of their meals at the condo.

Feature: Weekly rental price includes unlimited use of three bicycles.

Benefit: Vacationers will save the $10.00 per day bike rental fee and be able to access all areas of the resort.

Target Your Market

You've analyzed your product. Now, let's target the market. Who are your potential customers? Review your property evaluation. Does your resort appeal to families, couples, or singles?

Look at the activities listed under your resort heading. Determine special interest groups who would want to visit your resort, such as skiers, fishermen, hunters, sailors, sunbathers, swimmers, backpackers and hikers,

CAUTION: Divided Highway Ahead!

How you divide the labor between you and your business partners is critical to your experience as a vacation property owner.

During our vacation, my wife and I cleaned our condo ourselves rather than have our rental management company provide the service. We saved a $50 cleanup charge and we did a very thorough job. All told, it took 4 hours of our time.

Taking away 4 hours of precious vacation time to clean a condo is not a good idea. It's insanity! We could have spent those 4 hours writing a flier and mailing it to 200 friends, business associates, and former renters, inviting them to reserve a week at our property for the upcoming season. Or we could have spent far less time strategically placing a classified ad in one or two weekly newspapers. If those marketing efforts resulted in two extra weekly rentals at $1000 each, we could have paid for 40 weekend cleanings by our rental management company!!

 Devote your time to marketing and enjoying your property. That's where you have the greatest return on your time and efforts.

Rely on your team of professionals (rental manager, accountant, interior design firm, real estate agent, attorney, etc.). Use these experts to help you get the most from your resort property. Delegate other tasks and spend your own time using the dozens of techniques and tactics described in this book to locate extra renters – above and beyond what your rental manager gets for you. And, above all, remember to enjoy your property as much as you can. That's why you bought it in the first place!

I don't know the key to success, but the key to failure is trying to please everybody.
— Bill Cosby

antique collectors, historians, birdwatchers, bowlers, joggers, skin divers, and photographers. If you own property at a tennis resort, begin to think of ways to reach the membership of all the tennis clubs in your area. Or, if your resort features several golf courses, consider how to reach the golfers at the country clubs in your area.

Remember that you're selling a product and you won't sell many bathing suits to the Eskimos or snow shoes in the Caribbean.

Your weekly rental rate is probably the single most important factor in targeting your market. If you rent your vacation property for $1000 per week at a resort with gourmet restaurants and high greens fees on the golf course, you may find a good market for your product in the more exclusive suburbs of your city, at the country clubs, and in the higher paid executive and professional working ranks.

After you find out who and where the market is, it will be much easier to reach it. Think of Diogenes who spent days roaming the streets in search of an honest man. His task would have been so much easier if he had had some sort of a description.

Action Steps:

 List the features of your property, the resort, and the area.

 Translate the features into benefits for prospective renters in all communications.

 Determine the types of people most likely to rent your property so you may focus your promotion campaign in their direction.

Use Your Personal and Business Contacts

Just as a new insurance agent uses his relatives, friends, and acquaintances to build a client base, you can use the same strategy to develop a list of potential renters.

Talk to your parents, your brothers and sisters, your nephews and nieces, and your aunts and uncles. Would they like to rent your property? And – very importantly – do they know of anyone else who would?

Develop a listing of all your contacts, including names, addresses, phone numbers, fax numbers, and e-mail addresses.

Starting with your relatives, expand this list to include close friends, neighbors, school mates and college chums, business associates, and social acquaintances. Get names and addresses of the members of your aerobic dance class and the members of your adult education class. Consider purchasing a special address book (tax deductible) specifically for your resort property address listing. Or, better yet, create a special database containing this information that can then be used to prepare mailings or send out faxes.

People can be divided into three groups: those who make things happen, those who watch things happen, and those who wonder what happened. — John W. Newbern

Obtain membership directories to your clubs such as the Jaycees, or the Rotary, or the community women's club. Check your Yellow Pages for groups in your area. Look under organizations.

If you're not a member of a certain group, maybe you know people who belong. Talk to them. See if they can obtain a directory for you.

Many high schools and colleges put out alumni directories giving names, addresses and phone numbers of former students. Purchase a directory (tax deductible) and add it to the other listings of potential renters.

Go through all of the business cards you've accumulated over the years and, if they match the profile of a potential renter that you developed in Chapter 12, add them to your database and record their contact information.

Spend some evenings or weekends phoning potential renters in your area. Determine their interest in renting your property. Ask them if they have friends who are golfers, tennis players, or skiers, who might be interested. Obtain names and addresses for your address listing.

Remember that a vacation property is a long-term investment. You may have your resort property for 5, 10, or 20 years. The work you do now can pay dividends in property rentals for years to come, so it's well worth the effort.

Don't spend lots of money on a long distance phone call when you can send a letter via fax, e-mail, or "snail mail" for a fraction of the cost. Personal letters to out-of-state friends are a good vehicle, while a direct mail campaign to less familiar out-of-state potential renters might be a less time-consuming approach.

Action Steps:

 Use personal contacts to begin a list of potential renters.

 Add to your list with directories, business cards, and referrals.

Direct Mail to Special Interest Groups

Spread the word inexpensively to key special interest groups with a direct mail campaign. Direct mail provides the opportunity to capture a prospective renter's undivided attention – at least for a few seconds. Compare this with magazine or newspaper advertising, where readers may never see your ad among all the competition.

For example, if you have an alumni directory from your college, develop a letter and mail it to all of your old classmates and to alumni both in the classes preceding and following yours. Use your judgment to exclude names and addresses for geographic reasons. For example, if your resort is on the Atlantic coast, you might want to exclude class members with addresses west of the Mississippi.

If your resort specializes in tennis and golf, try to get a membership directory of all the tennis, golf, and country clubs in your area. Develop a special letter for the golfers and another for the tennis players. If possible, include a brochure or other promotional literature with your letter. Your resort might supply this material, or you might purchase a bulk supply from its sales and marketing department.

If you own a ski chalet, get a membership directory of the local ski club and reach each member directly with your letter.

Ask not what the renter can do for you, ask what you can do for the renter.

Build your letter around what happens to vacationers when they visit your property. The more you do this, the more likely they are to think of you when they want to vacation.

Direct mail can be an effective and inexpensive vehicle to reach prime candidates for your property rental. The more selective you are, the more successful you will be in the response to your campaign. Remember the target market profile you developed earlier (see Chapter 12). Always weigh the expenses and time involved in mailing against its probable success.

Your mailing costs are currently 32 cents per letter, or $32 per hundred. You can have your letter duplicated at one of the many fast printing outlets. If you are not using a word processing program or you are not comfortable with the mail merge function of that program, you might consider using a secretarial service to address the envelopes from your directory. It's another tax-deductible expense, and it might speed up the project.

Action Steps:

 Target a group that has an interest in the features of your resort.

 Develop a letter for the members of that group, outlining those features.

 Try to obtain promotional literature from your resort to send with your direct mail letter.

 Use the following "Sample Document" as a guide to preparing your direct mail piece.

Sample Document

Dear Tennis League Member:

If there were a way that you could spend your next vacation at one of the country's newest and finest tennis resorts, you would be interested, wouldn't you?

Then consider these facts about Crystal Sands Resort, SC:
- 20 clay courts, 5 lighted hard courts for night play
- Organized instructional tennis programs, including lessons from top pros
- Daily round robins, weekend singles and doubles tournaments, stroke-a-day clinics, ball machines and practice alleys
- Tennis hostess on duty from 9 a.m. to 5 p.m. to help you arrange matches with players of equal talent

In addition to a top-flight tennis program, Crystal Sands offers:
- Five miles of uninterrupted Atlantic Ocean beach for swimming, sunning, sailing, fishing...and relaxing.
- Three championship golf courses to delight and challenge handicappers of all levels.
- Gourmet dining, bike trails, guided nature walks, and sightseeing to make your vacation complete.

Our one-bedroom deluxe villa will provide luxurious accommodations while you enjoy the beauty and the activities of Crystal Sands. Fully furnished with vaulted ceiling and a screened-in porch, the villa has a color TV, washer and dryer, and a queen-size bed. Furnishings include all the linens, towels, and dishwares you need, right down to the corkscrew for your complimentary bottle of wine. To make your vacation just a little nicer than you expect, we will send you a $50 rebate check at the end of your visit. Call Chris Cain, 407-555-1111 for rates, reservations, and more information.

Christopher S. Cain
1007 Green Branch Court
Oviedo, FL 32765

* Crystal Sands Resort, SC, is a fictitious name used only as an example of a typical vacation resort.

Fliers to Your Neighbors

It's time to try some magic. Take away the postage stamp. Take away the envelope. And presto! Your direct mail piece (from Chapter 14) turns into a flier or handbill.

Because you're not paying postage and addressing envelopes, a flier is a simple, quick, and inexpensive vehicle to get your message to the marketplace. Type your message. Have it printed. Distribute it.

One consideration: Since you're distributing the flier to a broader audience (e.g., all of the neighbors in your housing complex), expect fewer responses.

To reflect this broader audience, modify the copy that you used in your direct mail letter. Instead of beginning "Fellow Fisherman" or "Dear Tennis Club Member," you might begin your flier with "Dear Neighbor," or "Dear Lakeside Village Resident."

Take a method and try it. If it fails, admit it frankly, and try another. But by all means, try something.
— Franklin D. Roosevelt

Highlight all the major features of your resort and your property. One neighbor might rent because of the golf at your resort. Another might rent because of the beach and swimming pools.

If you're distributing the flier to all of your neighbors, consider using the neighborhood paper delivery person to distribute the fliers. Pay him/her with a check so you have a record of this tax-deductible expense.

A word of caution: There are regulations against using mail boxes and mail slots for anything but U.S. mail. It's best to leave the flier on the doorstep.

If you target an apartment building for flier distribution, talk to the building manager. Explain that you believe many residents in this building will be interested in your vacation property, and offer him a bottle of his favorite liquor or a commission on each resident who actually rents your property in exchange for his assistance.

Pass out the fliers to everyone in your office or plant. The flier gives your associates a permanent communication on the features of your property. They can discuss your property and the resort with their families without forgetting any of the details.

Tales From the Road...

I distributed fliers describing my resort property to the 500 neighbors who lived in my housing complex. I spent an hour writing the flier, $30 to print it, and another hour distributing it door-to-door.

As a direct result of this effort, eight neighbors called to inquire and two of them rented my one-bedroom condo for one week each. One of these neighbors liked the condo and the resort so much, he returned the following year. That meant three extra rentals at $700 per week, or $2,100 extra rental dollars in my pocket – money I would not have received had I left property rentals completely up to the management company. Not a bad return on investment.

Action Steps:

Develop and distribute a flier to large groups within your community.

Use the "Sample Document" as a guide in developing your flier.

Sample Document

March 29, 1998

Dear Oviedo Neighbor:

If there were a way that you could spend your next vacation at one of the country's newest and finest ocean resorts, you would be interested, wouldn't you?

Then consider Crystal Sands Resort in South Carolina. This seaside villa complex offers complete facilities for an exciting, active get-away trip including:

- 3 championship golf courses
- 20 clay tennis courts; 5 lighted hard courts
- 5 miles of uninterrupted Atlantic Ocean beach
- Bike trails, jogging, swimming, sailing, and guided nature tours

We invite you to reserve a week at our new one-bedroom villa, ideal for a couple, a couple with one or two children, or two or three single golfers/tennis players. Located 400 feet from the Atlantic Ocean beach, our fully equipped villa with vaulted ceiling and screened-in porch will provide luxurious accommodations for your vacation while you enjoy the activities and the beauty of Crystal Sands.

For reservations, rates, and a Crystal Sands brochure, call Chris Cain (407) 555-1111.

Sincerely yours,

Christopher S. Cain
1007 Green Branch Court
Oviedo, FL 32765

P.S. Ask about the special $50 rebate for our Oviedo neighbors!

* Crystal Sands Resort, SC, is a fictitious name used only as an example of a typical vacation resort.

Mini-Posters

You can display your message on bulletin boards in your office cafeteria, at your community center, at your church, or in the local supermarket with a mini-poster.

Take your best photograph from your last vacation at your property and have a photo lab make 8 x 10-inch color enlargements. Request a two-inch border at the bottom for your message. Order an appropriate quantity based on your estimate of how many posters you can place at key locations in your area.

A picture is worth a thousand words. — Anonymous

Of course, if you have the equipment and the know-how, you could scan the photo and create your own poster using the scanned image. Or you can photograph your property using a digital camera and simply download the image to your computer.

Consider several versions of your mini-poster if your resort has several major features:

- Use a photo of the golf course to develop a mini-poster for the country clubs in your area.

- A second photo of the tennis facilities at your resort will make a good mini-poster for the tennis clubs in your area.

- Find a dramatic photo of the beach. Use this poster at grocery stores, beauty parlors, and community centers.

Ask friends who work at businesses in your community to post your photo on the bulletin boards at their companies.

Know someone who works at a hospital? Ask them to place your mini-poster on the bulletin board in the doctors' executive dining room and in the nurses' lounge.

Action Steps:

 Use your best photographs to develop mini-posters.

 Use the "Sample Document" as a guide.

 Display your posters on bulletin boards in key locations.

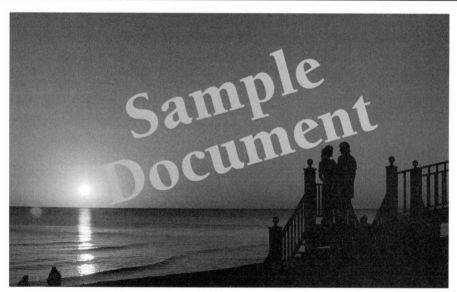

"Nothing Could Be Finer Than to Be in Carolina (Crystal Sands, SC) for Vacation"

Rent one-bedroom, furnished villa at $50 owner discount off the regular weekly Crystal Sands rate. Championship golf, tennis, gourmet dining, 5 miles of beach, shelling, fishing, and guided nature tours. Contact Chris Cain for details (407) 555-1111.

Caper At Cape Cod

Spacious, two-bedroom Cape Cod condo will provide luxurious accommodations for your next vacation. Fully furnished, sleeps six, dishwasher, color TV, two minutes from ocean, fishing, fine dining, sightseeing, bike riding. A true value for your vacation dollars. Call (508) 555-2222.

Coupon Power

Do you clip coupons? Many people do. Why? Coupon clippers save money on everything from food to film, from razors to car rentals.

Why not develop a coupon for your resort property? There are several good reasons why you should:

- A coupon catches peoples' attention because they view coupons as having a monetary value (which, of course, they do) whether it's 20 cents off a box of cereal or two dinners for the price of one.

- People tend to hold on to a coupon (hence the name: Coupon Clippers). If they don't use the coupon themselves, they might pass it along to a friend or relative.

- You can use the coupon as a collateral piece to draw attention to your other materials, such as direct mail or fliers. When you display your mini-poster at the local tennis club, you should also give the club manager a supply of coupons to distribute to interested parties.

Make your coupon look like money and use it to attract attention to your special offer: $50.00 off a week's rental; seven days for the price of six; a free round of golf with a week's rental; or a free bottle of champagne with a week's rental.

The ad worked because it attracted the right audience... because it aroused curiosity and because it offered a reward.
— John Caples

The offer should be urgent, personal, and easy to understand. Think about what would make you drop everything and run. Be sure to describe exactly how a renter can take advantage of the offer, and tell them to do it. Don't be shy about urging people to "Call Now." It works.

Enlist the aid of a graphic artist (if you know one) to help design the coupon. Or you can get stock art at a graphic design supply house to make your coupon look more official. Or you can use your laser printer to print the text of the coupon on specialty color paper stock, giving it the look of a four-color print job for a fraction of the cost.

Leave space for the potential renter's name, address, phone number, fax number, and e-mail address so you can add the information to your listing. Conversely, make sure your phone number, e-mail address, and/or Web page information appears on the coupon so the renters may easily contact you.

How do you know which idea works best? Print two different offers and code them so that you know when you get an inquiry whether the renter responded to the special rate, the extra day, or the free champagne. Stick with the most successful offer on subsequent printings.

Action Steps:

 Develop a coupon which advertises and offers a discount on your resort property.

 Obtain stock art or lettering stencils to make your coupon appear professional.

 Distribute your coupons as part of your other techniques (e.g., direct mail, brochures, etc.).

 Use the following "Sample Documents" as guides to prepare your coupons.

$50   **$50 Off** $50
**the weekly rental
for one-bedroom deluxe villa**
at 100 Ocean View Drive, Crystal Sands Resort, SC

(Availability Permitting – March 15 through November 15, 1999)
For details and reservations, call Chris Cain
$50   **(407) 555-1111** $50

FREE   **FREE**   FREE
Round of Golf for Two Including Cart
at Crystal Sands, SC
With week's rental of one-bedroom deluxe villa at 100
Ocean View Drive, Crystal Sands Resort, SC

(Availability Permitting – March 15 through November 15, 1999)
For details and reservations, call Chris Cain at **(407) 555-1111**

Fact Sheets and Brochures

Beg, borrow, or buy bulk quantities of brochures from your resort. Don't underestimate the value of a good brochure to your marketing and publicity efforts. They're usually colorful and dramatic. They're permanent.

Remember that brochures currently, and in the past, have been the single most widely used method of promoting resorts. Visit any travel agency and you'll find hundreds of brochures on display.

If you think you can use 50 brochures in your efforts, you probably can use 500...or even 1,000. And, while you're at it, see if you can get a promotional video featuring your resort.

Most management companies will be happy to supply an owner who is aggressively promoting the resort with supplies of brochures and video tapes.

Life is a continuous exercise in creative problem solving.
— Michael J. Gelb

- It shows management support for the owners, the investors who help assure the success of the resort.
- Every vacationer who rents the owner's property spends money for food and beverages and on recreation, such as golf greens fees, and tennis court charges.

Once you've obtained the brochures, here are some of the many ways you can use them:
- Send them with your direct mail piece to special interest groups.
- Distribute them to co-workers at the plant or office.
- Send them with letters to your friends.
- Leave a supply with the tennis club manager, the beauty shop owner,

or the health club front desk.

- Always keep a supply in your briefcase or coat pocket to pass out whenever you encounter a potential renter.
- Mail them to all interested parties as a follow-up to inquiries.

A resort brochure gives prospective renters an overview of the resort, its features and activities, and usually some highlights of the surrounding area.

You can also collect promotional materials of the big spenders in your area – the chamber of commerce, department of tourism, big hotels or motel chains. Analyze the way they sell the area. This can give you a good idea of why people come to your community. And you can then highlight those features in your own promotional materials.

But, what about your property? Anyone interested in renting will have dozens of questions regarding:

- The weekly, daily, or monthly rental price
- Location within the resort
- Furnishings
- Security
- Check-in/check-out time
- Management company phone number in case of malfunctions
- Owner's home phone and address in case of an emergency
- Phone number on the property
- Special instructions

Put yourself in the position of a future renter. What would you want to know if you were vacationing in a rental property? With a Fact Sheet, you can give prospective vacationers this pertinent information before they leave home. The Fact Sheet can save time and help to avoid problems and misunderstandings.

On the flip side of your Fact Sheet, copy a map of your resort and indicate your property location and other key points, such as your management company office.

You can update your Fact Sheet from year to year with little effort. Then copy or print an adequate supply and send them out with your brochure in response to all inquiries. Make sure that anyone who rents your property receives a Fact Sheet before their trip.

You will also want to leave a supply of the Fact Sheets at your property in case someone forgets to bring their advance copy along.

Action Steps:

 Obtain a quantity of brochures and video tapes on your resort.

 Distribute the brochures (with your other literature) to all prospective renters.

 Write a Fact Sheet with details about your property.

 Use the "Sample Document" as a guideline to develop your Fact Sheet.

 Distribute your Fact Sheet to prospective and confirmed visitors to your property.

Sample Document

Fact Sheet to Prospects and Confirmed Renters

100 Ocean View Drive
Crystal Sands, S.C. 50000

One-bedroom unit on second floor of a two-story, eight-unit building.

Built in 1996 – purchased new; central air conditioning and heating.

Fully furnished – includes all linens and kitchen utensils.

One-minute walk to beach; two-minute walk to new Olympic pool and children's pool; five-minute walk to tennis courts and golf course.

Back of villa overlooks a lagoon.

Living Room/Kitchen
- Cathedral ceiling with exposed wooden beams.
- Full-size appliances including stove, refrigerator with ice maker, dishwasher, garbage disposal, and toaster, electric mixer, blender, iron and ironing board, coffee maker, food processor.
- Zenith color TV and radio.
- Simmons double hide-a-bed (sleeps two)
- All-glass wall with sliding doors faces the screened-in porch that contains a glass-top table with four chairs.
- Washer and dryer.

Bedroom
- Queen-size bed (firm mattress).
- Dresser, mirror, and night stand.
- Villa telephone – (xxx) xxx-xxxx.
- Walk-in closet.

Property Management Company – Resorts Management, Inc., 500 Center Street, Crystal Sands, SC, 50000. Contact: Gene Robinson, rental manager; hours: 8:00 a.m. to 8:00 p.m. daily.

The management company is at your service 24 hours a day for any emergency. Check-in time is 4:00 p.m. and check-out is 11:00 a.m. Resorts Management, Inc. will clean the villa upon your departure. If you wish an additional clean-up during your visit, the charge will be $30.

For ambulance, police, or fire department, dial 911.

Property Owner: Chris Cain, 1007 Green Branch Court, Oviedo, FL 32765

Villa key is picked up and dropped off at management company. Balance of rent due is to be paid to management company upon arrival. The management company will mail cleaning and security deposits to renter's residence following a post-occupancy inspection assuming no damage or offsets are required.

---

* Crystal Sands Resort, SC, is a fictitious name used only as an example of a typical vacation resort.

Classified Advertising

The good news is, it *pays* to advertise. The bad news is, you *pay* to advertise.

Make sure that your "cost-effective" advertising actually increases your rentals. Since you're paying for it, you can advertise anywhere you choose – television, radio, or roadside billboards. But from a practical standpoint, we recommend classified advertising in the following print media:

Daily Newspapers. Place your ad in the *Resorts* or *Vacation* section of the classifieds and use the Sunday edition to reach the largest audience.

Suburban Weeklies. These are usually less expensive than larger dailies and you can select those newspapers that circulate in the neighborhoods where your target audience resides.

Magazines. Many metropolitan areas have "City Magazines" on the people, places, culture, and activities of the area. These publications tend to linger on the household coffee table long after the newspapers have been discarded, giving your message a lengthened life. Public Broadcast Station (PBS television) membership magazines are also an excellent place to advertise because of the higher demographics of individuals who contribute money to become members.

I know half of my advertising is wasted but I do not know which half. — William Wrigley

Area Advertisers. Looking for low classified rates? Check into some of the many area advertisers. They're usually inexpensive, and, as with the weekly newspapers, you can select those publications that serve neighborhoods where you would most likely find potential renters. Every city and every community has different newspapers, magazines and other advertising vehicles that we encourage you to explore.

For example, you might advertise in the program for your city symphony series. Weekly business journals provide a nice advertising vehicle since they circulate to executives and managers. Perhaps you can advertise in a weekly or monthly entertainment guide in your area.

Look at the activities on your resort list. There are dozens of magazines specializing in boating, skiing, skin-diving, tennis, golf, camping, and backpacking.

Classified advertising in national magazines tends to cost more, so select your publications carefully. Visit a bookstore with a wide selection of consumer magazines and you can get a better idea of the publications available. You can also check Bacon's Publicity Guide (at your local library) for a complete listing of all the magazines in the country.

Check your Yellow Pages for a complete listing of newspapers and magazines in your area.

Once you've selected some publications which you believe will reach potential renters, it's decision time because now you must ask yourself the following questions:

- How much do you want to spend on classified advertising?
- When do you want your ads to appear?
- How often do you want your ads to appear?

How much should you spend on classified advertising?

We suggest an advertising budget of approximately 10 percent of your projected gross rental revenues. You might increase this percentage if you're just getting started and have a poor occupancy rate.

You might decrease the percentage if you have a high occupancy rate and get many of your rentals through other methods, such as direct mail, family referrals, or repeat business, or the dozens of other techniques outlined in this book.

For example, if your villa rents for $1,000.00 per week and you're shooting for 30 weeks of rentals, consider an advertising budget of $3,000.00.

Or, if your condo rents for $500.00 and you're trying to increase your rentals this year to 34 weeks (gross rental revenues: $17,000.00), try a budget of $1,700.00.

If these figures sound high, remember:

- Any travel agent would charge a resort approximately 10% to refer a renter.
- You can pay for your entire advertising budget with several new renters that result from your ad campaign.
- You may be able to decrease this budget in years ahead as your rental occupancy rate increases.
- Advertising and promotion expenses are tax deductible.

Tales From the Road...

You might do well to advertise in a few of the many specialty magazines, if they reach your target audience. For example, because my resort has an excellent airstrip nearby, I advertised in a monthly flying magazine, resulting in several rentals to pilots.

When should your ads appear?

Run your ads when vacationers plan their trips. Most people vacation during the summer, especially if they have school-aged children. Generally, you should advertise in the late winter and during the spring to reach these people. Many people like to "get away" for the holidays including Thanksgiving, Christmas, and New Year's. You can reach them with advertising in October and November. If you have a winter "Off Season," try some special ads during November and December to attract residents of northern cities interested in escaping the cold with a longer term rental (two weeks, a month, two months, etc.).

How often should your ads appear?

Your budget will dictate the frequency. But, you might get lower advertising rates if you run your ads for consecutive weeks or months. In this way, you can get more bang for your advertising dollar and you can save on your time, since you place the ad only once.

One final note on advertising:

Measure the effectiveness of your campaign by logging all of your inquiries. When someone calls about your property, ask them where they saw the ad. Based on this information, you can discontinue an ad in a publication that is not producing inquiries, and beef up your efforts in the publications that are generating a good response. Save the names and contact information from any respondents to your marketing and add that information to your mailing list.

Action Steps:

 Select one or several key publications for classified advertising.

 Plan and budget your advertising campaign.

 Keep close track of your marketing efforts and ask all renters and callers how they heard about your property. If you don't see the return from a particular ad or approach, stop spending money on it.

Company and Organization Newsletters

You can extend your classified advertising campaign to reach more of your target audience by using company and organization newsletters. And this time the news is all good because usually you don't have to pay for this type of advertising.

If you work in a plant or a large company office, your corporation or company probably publishes a weekly, monthly, or quarterly newsletter.

Some communities, apartment complexes, credit unions, clubs, and organizations also publish newsletters, and if you're a member of the group, you can usually place a classified advertisement free of charge.

If I have a thousand ideas and only one turns out to be good, I am satisfied.
— Alfred Nobel

The price is right, so scout around for as many newsletters as possible. Use your network of friends, relatives, and associates and ask them to list your classified ad in their newsletters at work or in their special interest group newsletters.

Action Step:

 Place your classified ad in company and organization newsletters.

Build a Sales Force 21

Regional Representatives

If you live in Louisville and own resort property in Florida, consider setting up a regional sales force. Use your brother in Baltimore, your sister in Chicago, and your uncle in New York City to help you rent your property. Perhaps your college roommate now lives in Chattanooga or your associate at work transferred to Washington, D.C.

Interest your friends and relatives in serving as regional sales representatives for your resort property. They can promote your villa or condo in their city as part of your overall marketing strategy.

Make sure each of your sales reps has copies of your promotional literature including:
- Fliers and handbills
- Mini-posters
- Coupons
- Brochures

Note: You probably do not want to distribute the fact sheets because you should use them in response to inquiries generated by your sales force and your publicity and advertising programs.

If any member of your sales force locates a potential renter, have the inquiry funneled to you so that you can handle the reservations with your management company. That gives you control and prevents any double bookings or other scheduling problems.

I get by with a little help from my friends.
— John Lennon

Pay your sales reps on a commission basis – 10 percent is standard – or pay them a set fee ($30.00, $80.00, etc.) for each referral that results in a paid vacation at your property.

You might prefer to keep all of the rental revenues and offer your regional sales force a free week's vacation at your property in exchange for a set number of referrals.

Talk to the Travel Agent

Approximately three out of four Americans who plan a vacation use a travel agency for assistance, recommendations and reservations.

Do you currently use a particular agency for airline reservations and other travel arrangements? Have you used an agency in the past? Do you know any travel agents in your community?

If you answered yes to any of the above three questions, you have an inside track on "talking to the travel agent."

Your strategy: Contact travel agents and ask them to steer business your way. Offer to pay the agent the prevailing commission for his/her service just as a major hotel chain might contract the agent to promote its properties. Plan to spend a few lunch hours talking to various travel agents in your city.

I no doubt deserved my enemies, but I don't believe I deserved my friends.
— Walt Whitman

You may be surprised at how receptive the agents are towards your proposal – and why not? They will get paid from you just as they will from a major resort. And your property might be exactly right for a couple or a family inquiring about a vacation in your area. Show the agent your photo album. Leave a supply of brochures, fact sheets, and coupons.

Work With Your Local Realtor

Your local Coldwell Banker office or the office of the real estate company who sold you your vacation property is another excellent networking resource. Often, vacation property buyers choose to rent for a season or two to confirm that an area meets their lifestyle. In the case of Coldwell Banker Resort Property Network™ offices, sales associates keep records on prospects interested in making a future purchase of a vacation home in the area. This can be an additional partner with whom to work closely to find more rentals.

Host a Wine and Cheese Party

Once you have used some of the other techniques described in this section to generate interest in your property, you might find it advantageous (and enjoyable!) to address potential renters as a group, rather than individually.

Assemble a group of interested people - friends, neighbors, or associates who might be interested in renting your property.

Try an informal wine and cheese party and use the occasion to inform your potential renters about your new product developments.

Distribute your promotional literature, including brochures, fliers, and mini posters. Show a promotional video featuring your resort or circulate your photo album. Explain the rental rates, any discounts or special promotions for potential renters.

A wine and cheese party, a cocktail party, or a variation thereof is a nice way to gather your prospects to give them information about your property. It adds credence and structure to your business operation. It can be an enjoyable event, and it's tax deductible.

Action Steps:

 Use relatives, friends, and associates to help you promote and rent your property.

 Talk to travel agents and arrange to have them refer business to you in exchange for a commission.

 Work with your local real estate agent as an additional partner for finding more renters.

 Hold informal parties for your potential renters.

Other Owners Can Help

When you see a fellow resort property owner advertise in the local newspapers, don't look at the ad as competition...something which will take potential renters away from you. The market for renting resort property is huge, with rentals for everyone who is willing to expend a little effort.

That resort property owner can be more of an ally than a competitor. So, call him/her to exchange information on your respective investments. Ask the owner:

- Who manages their property?
- What commission does that management company charge?
- Have there been any problems with the property?
- What was the occupancy rate last year?
- How do the prospects look for this year?
- What is the weekly rental?
- The daily?
- The monthly?
- Is there a special off-season rate?
- How does he/she advertise?
- Who cleans the condominium or villa?
- What is the charge per cleaning?
- Who distributes the keys to visitors and who handles security?
- When the owner visits his/her property, does he/she fly, drive, take a bus, or train?
- Are there any exceptional restaurants in the resort area?

Another owner might be handling his/her business more efficiently than you. You can learn from other owners and the information can result in substantial savings.

Your biggest benefit in contacting other owners is the establishment of a reciprocal referral system.

If you have an apple and I have an apple and we exchange these apples, then you and I will still each have one apple. But if you have an idea and I have an idea and we exchange these ideas, then each of us will have two ideas. — George Bernard Shaw

Suppose the other owner has a three-bedroom condo and you own a one-bedroom condo. When you receive calls from parties requiring more space than a one-bedroom unit, refer them to the other owner. And ask the other owner to return the favor.

Even if you and the other owner both own one-bedroom units, there will be occasions when your condo is booked for the week when the potential renter would like to visit. Refer the caller to the other owner and, hopefully, the other owner will reciprocate.

Form a Club for Property Owners

While you're publicizing your property as an individual, perhaps you can publicize your resort as a group. Get in touch with the other property owners from your resort who have their permanent residence in your area and form a club: the Virginia Beach Club of Baltimore, the Myrtle Beach Club of Cincinnati, the Nashville Hilton Head Club, or the Aspen Club of Chicago.

As a group, you can achieve the common goals of all the members: Promote your resort and increase the occupancy rates of everyone's properties. As a group, you'll have greater financial resources and the energies and talents of all the members. Cooperative marketing with other owners can increase your visibility and multiply your promotional dollar. Besides, it may even be fun.

Elect officers and plan club activities. A few ideas:
- Hold a winter party for all members and their guests (potential renters). Raffle a free trip to the resort to generate interest. Show a video or a slide show of the resort (get all of the club members to pool their best slides). Keep the business portion of the program brief – parties are for having fun.

- Sponsor a charter flight or bus for a special Spring Getaway, a Thanksgiving Weekend, or a Summer Golf or Tennis Extravaganza. Any of these charters can provide low-cost transportation for owners, their friends, and other renters. Low cost and convenient transportation can be added incentive for someone to rent your property.

- Take out a full-page ad in your area newspaper to promote your resort. List all the members of the club who care to rent their property with their phone numbers. The listing might also be according to the types of property – one, two, or three bedrooms – or according to price range of the weekly rentals. Check with the newspaper to see if they plan a spring vacation supplement. This might provide a good place for you to place your ad.

- Getting to know the other resort property owners in your area might provide reason enough for forming a club. The club can provide a forum of information on activities, restaurants, sightseeing, and shopping in your resort area.

Club members can exchange information on cleaning services and management companies. If you plan to redecorate your condominium, perhaps other club members can give you advice from their past experience.

Perhaps a club member plans a weekend trip to the resort in his private plane and has two extra seats he would like to fill. With the club, he easily can find other owners to travel with him.

A property owners club can provide both an enjoyable social function and a practical business experience.

Action Steps:

 Contact other owners in your area.

 Set up a referral system with them.

 Form a club of the owners at your resort who live in your area.

Riding on the Information Superhighway:

Put the Power of the Internet to Work

The Internet. It's not a fad. It's the beginning of the next business revolution that will affect the way we live, work, and play for the rest of our lives. Current projections say there will be over 100 million Internet users in less than four years, and one billion users in less than eight years.

Some 6 million travelers booked trips on-line in 1997 and the percentage of travelers who use online services and/or the Internet for travel plans or reservations jumped from 11% in 1996 to 28% in 1997. In 1998, the number of travelers booking on-line should increase by 12.1 million, according to the Travel Industry Association of America.

The information highway is being built and we know: We can be part of the steamroller or part of the road. — Dan Poynter

When you consider the sheer number of potential renters you can reach via the Internet, maintaining a Web site to promote your vacation property can be a reasonably cheap and effective marketing tool. If the prospect of creating a site on your own for just your property seems intimidating, perhaps you could persuade your property management company and/or the property owners association in your resort to participate.

Many local real estate companies, including Coldwell Banker, offer seasonal or vacation property rentals on their local Web sites. Coldwell Banker will be introducing a component to their international Web site in the future to support vacation rentals nationally and internationally. When completed, vacation rental properties from any resort market can be viewed on this award-winning Internet site that routinely enjoys several million contacts weekly from Internet users all over the world. Visit Coldwell Banker Online™ at www.coldwellbanker.com.

Where to Begin?

Do you need to understand the technical details of how your microwave oven works before you can cook a frozen entree? No.

Do you need to understand the technical details of how the Internet works before you can use it to market your property? No.

Don't get sidetracked by the high-tech aspect. Remember, the Internet is nothing more than a new medium for an old game: marketing. And the same rules of marketing apply: know what you are offering, to whom, why, and with what benefit.

The first thing you will need to do is decide what information you want to include on your Web site and how that information should be arranged. One of the best ways to figure this out is to browse the Web and see what other vacation property owners and resort developments are doing.

Search engines – Altavista, SavvySearch, and Yahoo! to name a few – are the tools people use to find information on the Internet. No, these are not gasoline-powered devices! But rather, they are intuitive programs allowing you to type a few key words into a form field, and then send the program along its merry way, searching through millions of pieces of computer stored information. In just a matter of seconds or minutes, the program will find and return those Web pages that include text matching or closely matching your key words.

> *When it comes to the information highway, we're roadkill.*
> — Gilbert F. Casellas, head of the Equal Employment Opportunity Commission lamenting his division's lack of computerization

Use one of these search engines yourself to look around and see what you find when you enter keywords related to vacation property rentals and your resort. Look at the pages of other vacation property owners, property managers, or resort development companies to get a feel for what you like or don't like about their sites.

What to Include

Think of your Web site as an electronic brochure for your vacation property. The first page should contain all of the essential information, including a brief summary of the features of your resort in general and of your property in specific.

From there, you can set your site up so that visitors can link to the details. For example, there could be a complete fact sheet on your property. Another section could list the recreational activities available at the resort, nice restaurants in the area, or any other information that might lure a potential renter to your property. You could show photos of your property (but not too many – remember the time it takes to transfer large photo files across your potential renter's telephone line!). Or you could have a map showing exactly where the resort is located and providing

 CAUTION: Two-Way Traffic Ahead

The world is shrinking every day. If you are only marketing your property locally, you are truly limiting yourself. The Internet offers a two-way means of communicating with prospective renters around the world.

Let's assess or track where my rentals came from. Most of the rentals I got during 16 years of ownership at Kiawah Island came from the Southeast. And my rental management company secured most of them.

However, we got many rentals from the Northeast: from Chicago, Cincinnati, Pittsburgh, Cleveland, and Washington, DC.

But that's not the whole picture. I also got a week's rental from a British couple who went to Kiawah to see the Ryder Cup Golf Tournament in 1991. Several years later, I rented my condo to a lady from San Francisco for an entire month.

TIP *Rentals can and do come from all over the country and from other countries around the world. The Internet provides a global reach to 60 million consumers in 40 countries around the world. Those potential renters can access the Internet and the Web site that showcases your vacation property 365 days a year, 24 hours a day.*

The Internet has revolutionized advertising and it is the perfect media for buying, selling, and renting any vacation property.

instructions on how it can most easily be reached (nearest airport, etc.).

By all means, include a price list, but make sure that it is updated to reflect your current rates. You may even want to consider including a discount coupon on your Web page to help you measure the effectiveness of your Internet marketing activities.

An on-line reservation form is an excellent idea. Once someone has found your site and becomes interested in your property, don't make them jot down a telephone number, go off line, and place a phone call! Instead, allow them to click on your e-mail address and send a message right then and there.

If you really get into it, you could also develop pages in which you tell about the history of the area in which your property is located, describe interesting festivals, cultural events, or human interest stories. If you have the time and the inclination, you can create an interesting and informative site that people will want to come back to over and over again.

Constructing Your Site

All Web pages are written in a specific code language called Hypertext Markup Language (HTML). Luckily, that's all you need to know about it. If you

Thousands of Web sites, including the Coldwell Banker Web site (www.coldwellbanker.com), showcase real estate on the Internet.

are interested in "doing it yourself," you can use an HTML editor, such as HotDog or FrontPage, to create your pages. Alternatively, most word processing software packages now have the ability to output your documents as HTML, either built-in or by downloading a plug-in. These will work as long as you don't want too many complicated features. The good news is that this sort of tool is advancing so rapidly that it won't be long before you can do anything you want to with a simple point and click.

Most of what you need to know about simple and successful Web design you can learn from the Web itself – either by looking at existing pages and deciding what you like and don't like about them, or by going through one of the on-line tutorials on Web design. In general, use clear headings and concise language, use lots of white space and some (but not too many) pictures.

If cyberspace isn't your thing or if you feel that your time would be better spent doing something else, there are lots of companies out there that will be happy to create your pages for you. They charge an equally wide range of prices, so be sure to shop around. Perhaps you could even exchange a week at your property for a Web designer's services!

Finding a Home

Next, you will need to find a server on which to place your pages so they will be available to anyone on the Internet. If you are using a Web page design service, they may offer you a package deal together with server space and maintenance. But, if you are creating your own pages, you may need to shop around to give them a place to stay.

Most online services or Internet service providers offer their customers a space for their own Web pages, including facilities to upload pages and graphics. There is normally no extra cost associated with this. However, your space is limited and your Web address may be somewhat long and complicated.

If you are working with your property management company and/or the property owner's association, it may be worthwhile to rent your own virtual server. What's a virtual server? Essentially, it is someone else's server on which you are renting space. However, it is set up so that it appears to the rest of the world as though you have your very own server. You get plenty of space to store your Web pages, along with other advanced features such as a list server and an auto responder. The cost associated with setting up a virtual server is typically around $30 per month.

Registering Your Pages

Now that you have a presence on the Web, how can you ensure that potential renters can find you? Think of using the Internet like looking up a particular type of business in the yellow pages for a major metropolis. Now picture how thick this book would be if it included every business in the world! See how easy it is to get lost in the crowd?!

Register your pages with all search engines. There are Web announcement services that will do the work for you for a fee typically ranging between $20 and $100. If you rent a virtual Web server or use the service of a Web page design service, announcing your Web page may already be covered by your contract.

The best way to ensure that your page is included in a potential renter's search results is to put a concise description of the property containing most of the keywords that are important to you on your first page.

Keep It Updated

If you are going to have a Web page, it should be an integral part of your overall marketing approach. Don't put it out there and forget about it. It will grow stale and gather dust! Make sure you keep it up to date. And make sure your Web site address appears on all your e-mail messages, letters, brochures, business cards, fact sheets, mini-posters – everywhere you can possibly put it!

Action Steps:

 Consider adding a Web site promoting your property to your overall marketing strategy.

 Whether you do it yourself or hire a professional to create your Web site for you, keep your site current and include the site address on all promotional materials.

 If cyberspace isn't your thing, work with a property manager or local real estate company with a Web site for advertising vacation rentals (see the directory of Coldwell Banker Resort Property Network™ offices in Section 5 of this book).

Repeat Business –

A Base to Build On

As with any business, your first years will be the toughest because you won't yet have a customer base for your product. You have to build one using the techniques outlined in this book. But, if you have a good product at a reasonable price, your customers will return and they will refer their friends.

Ideally, you will reach a point in four, six, or perhaps ten years when you can cease your publicity and advertising efforts and rely solely on your repeat business and referrals to maintain a high occupancy rate for your property.

Then you will have truly maximized your investment because you will have achieved your high occupancy rate and eliminated publicity expenses. That is certainly an exciting vision of the road ahead!

Information/Welcome Kit

One thing you can do for your guests to enhance their stay in your property is to prepare an information kit and leave it in your unit. The information kit could include a personal letter of welcome from you, resort brochures, menus from local restaurants (with phone numbers and directions for how to get there), instructions for appliances (dishwasher, garbage disposal, washer/dryer, etc.), garbage pick-up days, community rules visitors should be aware of, a map of the area, etc.

You will have gathered this information as part of your own vacations on the property or as part of your efforts to attract additional rentals. Little touches such as this will make people want to come back to your unit time after time.

Guest Log

You can start a repeat business program with a guest log at your property. It doesn't matter if your management company or a travel agent originally referred renters to your property. Once they rent your property and sign your guest log, they're your customers.

And when the visitors return next year to again purchase your product, you have already paid the commission.

You can purchase a guest log for several dollars and up (tax deductible). Keep it prominently displayed in your unit and add the names and addresses to your permanent list of renters and potential prospects.

Thank You Notes

After someone rents your property, send a thank you note – a polite gesture of appreciation and a good business practice.

Keep your message simple and sincere:

> *Hope you enjoyed <resort name>. Thank you for your business. <Your signature>*

Add a P.S. if you like:

> *I welcome your comments on my property to help make it nicer for future renters.*

And enclose a stamped, self-addressed postcard.

Post Cards

Traditional direct mail promotions consist of a letter and possibly a brochure in an envelope. However, for your repeat customers, you might consider a self-mailing brochure, a newsletter (see below), or a well-designed post card. The Direct Marketing Association 1994-95 Statistical Fact Book indicates that a post card is the second most likely piece of mail to be read (after newspapers and magazines) and the *least* common piece of mail received. Post cards stand out.

Holiday Greeting Cards

The road to success is always under construction.
— Jim Miller

Use your list of all renters and potential renters to send holiday greeting cards. Like the thank you note, the greeting cards generate goodwill. And, again, keep your message simple and sincere.

Never use a greeting card for a commercial message. Your renters and potential customers will throw their cards straight into the Yuletide fire if they get a greeting such as:

Hope to see you next year at <resort name>.

We're offering a $50 rebate to previous renters next year on our condo.

But they will appreciate your holiday sentiments if you sign your card:

Yes, Virginia (Beach), there is a Santa Claus.

Merry Christmas from Myrtle Beach.

Sanibel sends Season's Greetings.

Greeting cards add a personal touch to your publicity program. It's these small extra steps that can make a big difference in your resort property investment.

Newsletters

Your thank you notes, post cards, and holiday greeting cards give you an opportunity to keep in contact with your customers in a non-commercial manner.

Get down to business and do some serious selling with a newsletter to these key customers and potential visitors. Use your newsletter to establish a communications link with your customers and to give them useful and enticing information.

Use your word processing or desktop publishing program to create your newsletter and then have it duplicated. You can use colored or specialty paper for a little extra flair. You can mail the newsletter to, for example, 100 past renters and potential prospects for $32 in postage.

That's not a bad investment considering that each newsletter might promote a return visit or generate a referral from your newsletter subscribers.

Send anywhere from one to four issues per year. Anything more than that and your newsletter could well cross the line from useful information to nuisance.

Regardless of the frequency, produce and mail your first issue in January or February, the time when most people begin to plan their vacations for the year.

Use this newsletter to announce your new prices for the year. If you're not raising them, point out to your readers that you're "holding the line on inflation to offer visitors true vacation value."

Explain your discount policy for previous renters and their friends. And explain your referral policy. Use this newsletter to describe any new features and improvements at your resort.

Another newsletter might highlight the top five or ten restaurants in the area. Get your readers involved. Include a recipe for a favorite dish from the area which your readers might prepare at home.

If you publish on a quarterly basis, highlight the seasonal activities at your resort and in the area, such as a concert series, a regatta, golf or tennis tournaments, etc.

Use one of the issues to promote your "off season." Send a newsletter which discusses the tremendous savings of an off-season visit. Emphasize the lower rates and the other benefits to vacationers:

- Uncrowded golf courses – no tee-off times required
- No reservations required at the area restaurants
- Shopping, sightseeing bargains
- Superb fishing
- Moderate climate – less humidity

Action Steps:

 Buy a guest log to record names and addresses of visitors to your property.

 Send a thank you note to everyone who rents your property and enclose a response card.

 Send holiday greeting cards to all previous and potential renters.

 Publish a newsletter for previous renters and potential visitors.

MAXIMIZING YOUR VACATION PROPERTY ENJOYMENT:

Remember to Have Fun!

What's the News Today?

Lying on his deathbed in 1899, Joseph Medill, the legendary American journalist is reported to have asked, "What's the news today?" The newspaper he bought in 1855, the *Chicago Tribune,* continues to report the news to this day. And Northwestern University's Medill School of Journalism continues to train scribes, writers, and media correspondents (including me...Medill class of 1971).

What is the news today? You can check the *Chicago Tribune* or your local paper, or you can check a host of electronic media outlets that did not even exist 100 years ago.

If you own a vacation property, consider subscribing to the newspaper in your resort area. If you own property in Myrtle Beach, SC, for example, subscribe to *The Sun News* (P.O. Box 406, Myrtle Beach, SC 29578-0406). If your property is in Aspen, subscribe to *The Aspen Daily News* (517 E. Hopkins, Aspen, CO 81611-1982). You own a condo in Key West? Subscribe to *The Citizen* (P.O. Box 1800, Key West, FL 33041-1800).

> **What's the news today?**
> — last words of Joseph Medill, American journalist

A daily subscription might be overkill. So perhaps you only order the Sunday issue and have it mailed to your home. Or perhaps you prefer to get the news online. Many newspapers have their own home page on the Internet. No matter which medium you prefer (paper or electronic) it's a good idea to keep up with the news in your resort area. The local paper will provide updates on restaurants, museums, cultural events, politics, shopping, and festivals.

All of this information can make your next vacation at your property more enjoyable. It may also be of use to you in creating promotional materials, such as newsletters, ads, etc. And you will be prepared when your renters ask, "Do you have any recommendations for a good place to eat?" or "Where can we go for some entertainment at night?"

News from your resort area will keep you informed on new road construction, economic development, political activities, new taxes, disasters such as hurricanes and beach erosion, festivals, and cultural events. You might want to clip and file articles such as the newspaper's annual guide to fine restaurants.

Need to Know

In early 1998, Coldwell Banker developed an intense, full day, accredited course for sales associates and brokers who sell vacation properties.

As part of the course, the company stresses the need to know specific details about your resort area and its amenities. The more you know, the better job you can do in selling property for your clients. Students are urged to find answers to the questions prospective buyers will ask.

Some examples from the course:

At an Ocean and Shoreline Resort
- Where is the public access to the beach?
- What is the cost of oceanfront property?
- Are there any bird or other wildlife sanctuaries?
- What are the swimming conditions?
  undertows/riptides?
  ocean temperature?
- Any marinas nearby?
- Are animals allowed on the beach?
- What type of shells can be collected?
- Size of waves?
- Sailing?
- Surfing?

For a Lake and Stream Resort
- Any boating restrictions?
- Are there piers and docks available?
- How about fishing and swimming?
- Hiking trails nearby?
- What is the depth of the lake/stream?
- Water temperature?
- Boat rentals and costs?
- Bike trails/rentals available?
- Restaurants and shopping in the area?
- What types of fish can you catch?

For a Golf Resort Area
- How many courses in the area?
- Greens fees?
- Any championship courses?
- Who designed the courses?
- Par & slope rating?
- Can you walk the course or carts mandatory?
- Advance tee times?
- Special twilight rates?
- Lessons available?
- Any outstanding teaching pros in the area?

For a Ski Resort Area
- What are the ski resorts within driving distance in the area?
- How many runs at each?
- Elevations and vertical drops?
- What is the longest run?
- Cost of a lift ticket?
- Average amount of snow?
- Average base depth?
- Best months to ski?
- Equipment rentals?
- How close is the major airport?

This is just a sampling of questions a prospective buyer might ask a sales agent or a broker. And it's important that the agent or broker know the answers. So they can sell the property!

If you want to rent you property, you also should know as much about your resort area as possible. Your potential renters will have plenty of questions about their vacation at your resort. If you know the answers...if you come across as an expert on the amenities at your resort area, you will increase your rental potential.

Action Steps:

 Subscribe to the newspaper that serves your resort area.

 Use the information for your newsletter and correspondence with potential renters.

 Use the information to enhance your vacations.

 Stay informed on the political and economic events of your resort area.

 Collect brochures, menus, magazines, fliers and other materials that contain information about your resort and its amenities. Keep a file of this material and take some time to learn specifics. It pays to know the answers to the questions your potential renters are sure to ask.

For your convenience, we've provided below the name, address, phone number, and home page address of newspapers in a sampling of popular vacation destinations across the continental United States. If your favorite vacation destination is not on the list, you can find this information in the reference section of your local library in Bacon's Newspaper Directory. Or contact the Coldwell Banker Real Estate office in your area of interest (see directory in Section 5 of this book). They will be happy to provide you with information about local newspapers, as well as other information about the community.

Arizona

Grand Canyon Country
Arizona Daily Sun, P.O. Box 1849, Flagstaff, AZ 86002-1849
(520) 774-4545

Phoenix - Valley of the Sun
The Arizona Republic, 200 E. Van Buren, Phoenix, AZ 85004-2238
(602) 444-8000 www.azcentral.com

California

Lake Tahoe
Tahoe Daily Tribune, P.O. Box 1358, South Lake Tahoe, CA 96156-1358
(916) 541-3880

Monterey - Big Sur
The Monterey County Herald, P.O. Box 271, Monterey, CA 93942-0271
(408) 372-3311

Palm Springs
The Desert Sun, P.O. Box 2734, Palm Springs, CA 92263-2734
(760) 322-8889

Yosemite - Sequoia - Death Valley
Mammoth Times Weekly, P.O. Box 3929,
Mammoth Lakes, CA 93546-3929
(760) 934-3929 www.mammothtimes.com

Colorado

Aspen
Aspen Daily News, 517 E. Hopkins, Aspen, CO 81611-1982
(970) 925-2220

Colorado Springs
The Gazette, P.O. Box 1779, Colorado Springs, CO 80901-1779
(719) 632-5511 www.gazette.com

Denver - Rocky Mountain National Park
Denver Post, P.O. Box 1709, Denver, CO 80201-1709
(303) 820-1010 www.denverpost.com

Connecticut

Mystic Seaport - Connecticut Valley
Mystic River Press, P.O. Box 187, Mystic, CT 06355-0187
(860) 536-9577 www.localnews.com

Florida

Marco Island
Marco Island Eagle, P.O. Box 579, Marco, FL 34146-0579
(941) 394-7592

Orlando - Space Coast
Orlando Sentinel, 633 N. Orange Ave., Orlando, FL 32801-1349
(407) 420-5000 www.orlandosentinel.com

Sanibel - Captiva Islands
Sanibel-Captiva Islander, Breeze Corporation, P.O. Box 56,
Sanibel, FL 33957-0056
(941) 472-5185

St. Augustine - Northeast Coast
The St. Augustine Record, P.O. Box 1630, St. Augustine, FL
(904) 829-6562 www.staugustine.com

Panhandle
Northwest Florida Daily News, P.O. Box 2949,
Fort Walton Beach, FL
32549-2949   (850) 863-1111

Idaho

Boise - Sun Valley
The Idaho Statesman, 1200 N. Curtis Road, Boise, ID 83706-1239
(208) 377-6200

Coeur d'Alene
Coeur d'Alene Press, P.O. Box 7000, Coeur D'Alene, ID 83816-1929
(208) 664-8176 www.cdapress.com

Maine
Bar Harbor

The Bar Harbor Times, Courier Publications, P.O. Box 249, Rockland, ME
04841-0249   (207) 594-4401

Massachusetts
Cape Cod

Cape Cod Times, 319 Main Street, Hyannis, MA 02601-4038
(508) 775-1200 www.capecodonline.com

Martha's Vineyard

Martha's Vineyard Times, P.O. Box 518, Vineyard Haven, MA
02568-0518
(508) 693-6100

Nantucket

The Inquirer and Mirror, P.O. Box 1198, Nantucket, MA 02554-1198
(508) 228-0001

Michigan
Mackinac Island - Sault Ste.Marie

The Evening News, 109 Arlington Street, Sault Ste. Marie, MI
49783-1942
(906) 632-2235

Montana
Glacier National Park - Flathead Lake

The Daily Inter Lake, P.O. Box 7610, Kalispell, MT 59904-0610
(406) 755-7000

Nevada
Las Vegas

Las Vegas Review-Journal, P.O. Box 70, Las Vegas, NV 89125-0070
(702) 383-0211 www.lvrj.com

New Jersey
Atlantic City

The Press of Atlantic City, 11 Devins Lane,
Pleasantville, NJ 08232-4107
(609) 272-1100 www.pressplus.com

North Carolina
Asheville - Smoky Mountains
Asheville Citizen-Times, P.O. Box 2090, Asheville, NC 28802-2090
(704) 252-5611 www.carolinamountains.com

Outer Banks
Wilmington Morning Star, P.O. Box 840, Wilmington, NC 28402-0840
(910) 343-2000

Ohio
Put-In-Bay - Lake Erie Shore, Ohio
Sandusky Register, P.O. Box 5071, Sandusky, OH 44871-5071
(419) 625-5500 www.funcoast.com

Oregon
Bend - Cascade Mountains
The Bulletin, 1526 NW Hill Street, Bend, OR 97701-1962
(541) 382-1811 www.bendbulletin.com

Coos Bay - South Coast
The World, 350 Commercial, Coos Bay, OR 97420-2269
(541) 269-1222

Crater Lake - Klamath Falls
Klamath Falls Herald and News, P.O. Box 788,
Klamath Falls, OR 97601-0320
(541) 885-4410

South Carolina
Charleston
The Post and Courier, 134 Columbus Street,
Charleston, SC 29408-4800
(803) 577-7111 www.charleston.net

Hilton Head
The Island Packet, P.O. Box 5727, Hilton Head Island, SC, 29938-5727
(803) 785-4293

Myrtle Beach
The Sun News, P.O. Box 406, Myrtle Beach, SC 29578-0406
(803) 626-8555 www.myrtlebeachaccess.com

Texas

Corpus Christi - Padre Island
Corpus Christi Caller-Times, P.O. Box 9136, Corpus Christi, TX
78469-9136
(512) 884-2011   www.caller.com

Utah

Salt Lake City
The Salt Lake Tribune, P.O. Box 867, Salt Lake City, UT 84110-0867
(801) 237-2800   www.sltrib.com

Virginia

Eastern Shore - Virginia Beach
The Virginia Beach Sun, Byerly Publications, P.O. Box 1327,
Chesapeake, VA 23327-1327
(757) 547-4571

Washington

Spokane
The Spokesman-Review, P.O. Box 2160, Spokane, WA 99210-2160
(509) 459-5000   www.virtuallynw.com

Wisconsin

Door County
Door County Advocate, P.O. Box 130, Sturgeon Bay, WI 54235-0130
(920) 743-3321

Wyoming

Yellowstone - Jackson - Tetons
Jackson Hole Guide, P.O. Box 648, Jackson, WY 83001-0648
(307) 733-2430   www.wyoming.com/~jhr/guide/

Trading Places:

Vacation Home Exchange

You're thinking about buying a vacation condo. You hesitate because you do not want to lock yourself into vacationing at the same spot for the rest of your life. It's like picking a favorite movie (e.g., Casablanca or Gone With the Wind) and then having to watch it 30 or 50 times. No, thank you!

Vacationing at the same spot year after year may become monotonous, no matter how beautiful the resort.

But, take heart. Vacation exchange provides a nifty solution. It's easy to expand your vacation horizons by trading places. Vacation exchange allows you to trade a vacation at your property for a vacation wherever you can locate one and convince the owner to trade.

Why not trade your vacation in Aspen for a week at a condominium in Aruba? Or trade a week of golf at Pinehurst for a week of skiing in northern Italy. Summer sun on the French Riviera...skiing in Colorado...deep-sea fishing on the Gulf of Mexico... vacationing in London, Hong Kong, or New York. These and thousands of other locations are available to those who join the world of vacation home exchange. Thousands of people exchange their homes every year and see their dream vacations come true.

But how do you find other owners willing to trade? It's not hard because about 6 million Americans own properties across the U.S. and in other countries. And owners from other countries maintain vacation properties around the world. In the U.S., there are roughly 4 million wholly-owned vacation properties and slightly less than 2 million households owning a timeshare.

There are also several organizations specializing in exchange services that will arrange trades for you:

Vacation Exchange Club, P.O. Box 820, Haleiwa, HI 96712

International Home Exchange (U.S. Affiliate of INTERVAC International), P.O. Box 190070, San Francisco, CA 94119

Vacation Link, P.O. Box 76350, Atlanta, GA 30358, 1-800-750-0797

Each of these organizations publishes one or more directories each year, listing thousands of properties in the U.S., Canada, and countries around the world whose owners are interested in a home exchange. Annual subscription fees run from $45 to $60, depending on the organization and whether or not you wish to list your property.

Timeshare Vacation Exchange

The timeshare industry has taken this type of trading to an art form. According to the American Resort Development Association (ARDA), the opportunity to trade your timeshare for vacations at other resorts is the number one reason consumers buy timeshares.

Resort Condominiums International (RCI) and Interval International (II) arrange the majority of trades for timeshare owners. RCI represents approximately 75% of the timeshare trading members worldwide, while II represents approximately 25%. There may be an advantage to having your timeshare property available to a larger population of members such as RCI's, but other service factors may influence your selection of which system to join as well. (For more keen insights, be sure and read the guest editorial on the timeshare industry written by Steve Miller of RCI, in Section 2 of this book.)

> *We live in a wonderful world that is full of beauty, charm, and adventure. There is no end to the adventures that we can have if only we see them with our eyes open.*
> — Jawaharlal Nehru

Resort Condominiums International, World Headquarters,
3502 Woodview Trace, Indianapolis, Indiana 46268-1104 (317) 876-1692, http://www.rci.com

Interval International, World Headquarters,
6262 Sunset Drive, Miami, FL 33143
(305) 666-1861, http://www.interval-intl.com

When you buy a timeshare, the company usually has an affiliation with either RCI or II, and many of the larger companies have exchange systems within their own resort complexes. For example, if you purchased a timeshare with Fairfield Communities, you could exchange your timeshare week in Orlando for a week at another Fairfield community, such as Branson, MO, Sapphire Valley, NC, or Pagosa Springs, CO.

Trading With Other Owners

Consumers who want to trade their wholly-owned vacation properties with other owners can arrange trades directly.

First, decide where you want to vacation: Myrtle Beach, SC, Sanibel Island, FL, Cape Cod, MA, Aspen, CO, Las Vegas, NV, Palm Springs, CA, Lake Tahoe, CA, Scottsdale, AZ, the Outer Banks of North Carolina, Branson, MO, etc.

Then, locate your exchange by watching the newspapers and magazines. Check the classifieds and, when you see someone renting a resort property in an appealing location, call him/her and make a deal.

Look at magazines such as *Sunset, Southern Living,* and others where you will find hundreds of other owners who have bought classified ads to rent their properties. Perhaps they would like to trade for a week at your resort. Select the property and resort. Call the owner. Arrange a trade. And guess what?! This type of trading doesn't cost you an annual fee or an exchange fee.

Other places to look for possible trades: vacation property Web sites, daily and weekly newspapers, city magazines.

Can you trade a week in your condo in Myrtle Beach for a timeshare

Tales From the Road...

At an auction following a charity golf tournament held several years ago, my friend Dan Peterson was the high bidder and subsequent purchaser of a weekend escape at the Chesterfield Hotel in Palm Beach, FL. When he invited his wife to take the trip with him, she said she would prefer a golf vacation.

When they mentioned this to me, I suggested that they trade me the Chesterfield weekend vacation for a week's accommodations at my villa at Kiawah Island, SC, one of the country's premiere golf and tennis resorts. The Chesterfield trip was shorter – just three days and two nights versus a full week in Kiawah – but their trip also included dinner for two at a gourmet restaurant and breakfast each day. So we called it an even trade.

The Peterson's reported a wonderful week of golf at Kiawah Island. My wife and I experienced a fantastic weekend getaway at the Chesterfield Hotel. And everyone went home happy.

week in Orlando? Sure you can. You own your condo. You are free to use it, rent it, trade it, donate it, or do whatever you want with it. A time-share owner can do whatever they want with their weeks as well – they just don't have as many weeks to choose from. As long as you can find someone willing to trade, you can make a deal.

Action Steps:

Rather than vacation at your own property each year, trade with other property owners around the world.

Locate other owners through newspapers, magazines, and the Internet.

Depending on the circumstances involved in exchanging or trading with vacation properties, there may be tax consequences. Readers should consult with their own legal or tax advisors to determine if tax consequences are an issue.

Advanced Trading

As we've discussed, you can trade one week at your property for one week at another owners property. But you can also take trading to a higher level and trade a week at your property for goods and services.

When you have weeks at your property that you are not renting or using, you can trade them. Let your imagination run wild. Make a list of goods and services you want and go after them. It can be lots of fun putting together a "trade" that is mutually beneficial. Look for "win-win" trading situations.

Golf clubs – Need a new set? Trade for them. The newspaper is filled with owners who want to sell their clubs. See if they will trade for a week's vacation accommodations. This trade is especially appealing to the owner of the golf clubs if your property happens to be at a golf resort – you already know they like golf.

Golf lessons – Contract with your local golf pro for a series of lessons in exchange for a week in your condo.

Attorney fees – You need a new will. Maybe your attorney needs a vacation. Maybe you can trade. Where there's a will, there's a way!

Massage therapy – Let's calculate this one. If your condo rents for $750 a week and your massage therapist charges $50 per hour, you could trade one week at the condo for 15 one-hour massage sessions. That's some serious stress reduction and relaxation, not to mention a fun and easy part of any overall fitness program.

Personal fitness trainer – Need some work on that waistline? Need someone to keep your fitness program on track? Trade the fitness trainer for his/her professional services.

Tales From the Road...

After I wrote Maximize Your Resort Property Investment *in 1984, I was asked to make a presentation to the National Association of Realtors® at its annual convention in Hawaii. I needed some coaching on my presentation and I needed help in adding visual aids to my speech — a few slides and graphics to illustrate my points.*

The solution was simple and, very importantly, cost-effective. I was able to get professional coaching from a long-time Westinghouse manager, Mr. Terry Smith, who has helped many executives improve and refine their presentations. Terry helped with my script and arranged for rehearsal at his home in front of a small group of his friends and neighbors. This allowed me to present my talk on my feet in front of a real audience.

Terry also provided ideas for graphic support, which included contacting a professional photographer in Baltimore. The photographer helped me get both bullet charts and beautiful color slides of resorts across the country to support my presentation.

To compensate both Terry and the photographer, I gave each person a week at my Kiawah condo.

Both men reported they had a delightful visit to Kiawah, and their help and assistance vastly improved my presentation in Hawaii. This was barter at its best.

Bon apetit – And after all that fitness training, you might want to reward yourself. Why not trade a series of gourmet dinners for a week at your property with the owner of your favorite restaurant?

Computer equipment – Trade for a printer, a monitor, a new or used computer, maybe even a joy stick for that new flight simulation package!

Computer tutor – Need help navigating your new computer system? Trade the computer tutor a week at your property for some sessions and lessons on your computer.

Dance lessons – A dance instructor might be delighted to help you and your spouse learn the latest dance steps in return for your vacation accommodations. It takes two to tango!

Furniture – What do you need? A sofa? Desk? Dining room table? Book case? Turn that vacant week at your condo into a new piece of furniture for your home with a trade.

Lawn services – Trade for the weekly mowing and edging of your lawn.

House cleaning – The owner

of a house cleaning service can provide you a series of cleanings in exchange for a week at your resort property.

Accounting services – You need help to keep your records straight and your tax returns on schedule. Find an accountant who will trade professional services for a vacation.

Graphic design/desktop publishing services – Need some help designing and producing the promotional materials for your vacation property (i.e., fact sheets, coupons, newsletters, etc.)? Find a graphic artist who is willing to help in exchange for a week's vacation.

I'll make him an offer he can't refuse.

— Mario Puzo, The Godfather

Web page designer – Not too keen on learning HTML or fooling with Web page editors? You may be able to swap a week's vacation with someone who will create your Web pages for you.

Need a new pet? – How about a Golden Retriever? Or a Chinese Shar-pei? Take the pick of the litter for a week at your resort.

Bartering is as old as the hills and the idea can work with virtually any good or service: artwork, instruments, music lessons, copying machine, cameras and camera equipment, camcorders, lawn mowers, antique furniture, air conditioning unit, washer and dryer, watches, jewelry, exercise equipment, aquariums, you name it.

Action Steps:

 Trade a week that would otherwise go unused for goods and services.

 Check with your accountant on the tax implications of trading.

Planes, Trains, and Automobiles

Getting to your vacation destination can be half the fun. What's the best way for you to visit your vacation property? Or, if you are renting a property at a resort for your vacation, what is the best way to get there?

Should you drive or fly? Why limit yourself to just those options? There may be other choices.

Consider some creative alternatives that just might make your trip more memorable, enjoyable, and exciting: How about a train? Hot air balloon? Ferry? Slow boat to China? Bobsled? Hydrofoil? The Space Shuttle? Horse and buggy? The Goodyear blimp? Harley-Davidson? Of course some of these options are in jest, but the point is, why wait until you get there to start having fun?! This is where the rubber hits the road!

Planes

Even if you don't know a pilot, you can charter a private plane. In certain situations, a charter plane can provide the ideal transportation to your vacation – even if the charter service has to drop you off and then pick you up a week later.

Trains

When was the last time you rode on a train? Amtrak routes criss-cross the entire continental United States. If one of them

> **Tales From the Road...**
>
> *In the 16 years that we've owned our vacation villa, we have lived in three different cities: Pittsburgh, PA, Columbia, MD, and Orlando, FL. We usually drive, but not always. Sometimes we fly into Charleston and rent a car. Fairly routine procedure.*
>
> *But once, we flew from Pittsburgh to Charleston in a private plane! One of our friends was a pilot and we split the cost of renting the plane. Now that was exciting!*

goes near your vacation destination, you might seriously consider this option. No traffic worries, for one thing.

When you come to a fork in the road, take it!
— Yogi Berra

For people on the Eastern Seaboard, there's the Amtrak Auto Train – the easy way to travel between the great vacation destinations of Washington, DC and Orlando, Florida. This is travel at its best! Load your car, van, or motorcycle into the enclosed car carriers at the end of the train, and then sit back in your comfortable seat or sleeping car for the relaxing 900-mile trip. Enjoy sumptuous meals (included in the ticket price), watch a movie, do a little star gazing, share a nightcap, or just stretch out and relax. Before you know it, you will have arrived at your destination, you'll be back in your own car and on your way to your ultimate destination. And you'll be well-rested and smiling.

Maybe you'd like to take the train but you don't have the time. Ask about Amtrak's Air Rail Travel Plan, which allows you to ride the rails one way and then fly back.

For more information, call Amtrak at 1-800-USA-RAIL (1-800-872-7245) or visit their web site at http://www.amtrak.com.

Automobiles

If you decide to drive, consider renting a car for the trip. Why not drive your own car? A spacious new rental car, like a Lincoln Town Car or a Cadillac, can add some sizzle and comfort to the trip.

Happiness isn't just around the corner, it is the corner!
— BMW advertisement

If the purpose of the trip is to check on your rental property, the rental charge may be tax deductible. And, of course, it keeps you from putting some heavy mileage on your own personal car.

Before you make an eight-hour drive to the seashore in a compact car with your wife and three kids, do yourself a favor and think about renting a full-size car or even a van. The trip will be much more pleasant and you will all arrive stress-free and ready to enjoy your vacation.

I took the road less traveled.
— Robert Frost

One of the advantages of driving is schedule flexibility. You can leave whenever you want. You can also stop along the way whenever you want. Why not plan to do just that? Rather than driving at breakneck speed for many long hours (arriving at your destination exhausted and irritable), why not take a more leisurely approach? Stay overnight at an interesting spot along the way. Take in a roadside attraction. Stop and smell the roses.

Action Steps:

 Compare travel options for your next vacation.

 Consider comfort, cost, and time.

 Consider the road less traveled if it adds fun and excitement to your trip.

Partners

If you don't believe you can handle the costs of a vacation property, don't give up the dream without considering another strategy. Consider a partner, or several partners.

At Kiawah, many of the properties were owned by partners and by small groups of partners. There is an entire spectrum of ownership possibilities between fully owning a vacation property and buying one week of timeshare:

Partners	Share	Access (in weeks)
2	$1/2$	26
3	$1/3$	17 $1/3$
4	$1/4$	13
5	$1/5$	10 $2/5$

Some developers are now selling quarter interests with 13 weeks of ownership each year per share. And in the timeshare industry there is a term for this – High End Fractional Shares – where buyers purchase large blocks of several weeks.

Anytime you decide to enter into a partnership, beware. This is no exception. Be sure to talk with your attorney and your accountant before taking action.

If you find yourself in a hole, the first thing to do is stop diggin'.
— Texas Bix Bender

However, a successful partnership can provide many benefits:

- You immediately divide investment costs by the number of partners.
- You multiply your publicity and marketing efforts by the number of partners.

It's better to own half a resort property that's 60% rented than to fully-own a property that's only 30% rented.

Action Step:

 As an alternative to selling your resort property, consider a partner to help pay expenses and assist in promotion.

Business Boosters

If Paul Simon could think of 50 ways to leave your lover, we should easily be able to come up with at least a few different ways to use your vacation property to boost your business.

If you own a business, you may have many opportunities to use your property to promote your business, increase sales, motivate and reward employees, and develop rapport and relationships with key customers.

There must be 50 ways to leave your lover. — Paul Simon

Using your vacation property for your business is a great way to break the monotony of repetitive daily tasks. Change the scene. Change the venue. Help stamp out business "burn out."

Let's give it a try. To get you started, here are ten ways to boost your business:

1. As an incentive, reward key employees by giving them the use of your vacation property (could be a weekend, a week, or longer).

2. Use your vacation property for your "Employee of the Month" program. For example, the monthly winner gets a week at your property on the company.

3. Hold staff meetings at your seaside property. Get out of the office and into a more relaxed and private environment. Employees will welcome a getaway, a business trip that breaks the routine. After your meeting and breakout sessions, get everyone to participate in a two-mile walk down the beach and back. Have lunch on the beach or on the deck at your vacation property.

4. Take your top management to your property to develop the strategic plan for next year. You can get a lot done without the interruptions of a busy office.

5. Reward your staff with a Super Bowl Party at your property.

6. Your vacation property might provide the ideal location for a holiday party for the staff.

7. Hold a customer meeting at your vacation property.

8. Schedule a weekend office barbecue at your beachfront condo, or your vacation home on the lake.

9. Hold your training session off-site at your vacation property.

10. You have delayed writing your speech for the upcoming annual convention for your industry's trade association. Get away from the interruptions of the office and plan a day or two by yourself at your vacation property to complete and rehearse your speech in the privacy of your favorite getaway.

> *The important thing is not to stop questioning.*
> — Albert Einstein

We've given you ten good suggestions. Can you think of more?

If you own a business and you are not using your property as an asset or marketing tool for that business, there's "no need to discuss much." "Just get on the bus, Gus. Make a new plan, Stan."

Action Steps:

 Use your vacation property to promote your business.

Donate a Week

For increased exposure of your vacation property investment (business) in your community, donate a week to a charitable cause. Donations may be made on a personal basis, or, if you own a business, in the name of your business or organization.

Your donation of a week can help raise funds for many worthwhile charities (American Diabetes Association, American Red Cross, Hurricane Relief Fund, local college or university, etc.), while at the same time creating a positive awareness of your company.

Often, a church, high school, or community organization raises funds by raffling prizes. Area businesses donate prizes to the organizations for recognition and goodwill. You can donate a trip to your property as a grand prize for the raffle.

If the public television or radio station in your community has an annual fund-raising "auction," donate a week. There's a publicity angle to this: Every time your property is mentioned on the air, potential renters hear about it. The station announcers will promote heavily the features of your resort. They will also give you credit for the contribution by name, making it easy for potential renters to get in touch with you. And every person who comes to your property free of charge as the result of a fund raiser will walk away as another satisfied customer to spread the word to other (paying) customers.

To help a good cause without hurting yourself, limit the availablility of your property to a slow time when it might otherwise be vacant. Track the way your donation is publicized, so that you can decide whether to do it again the next year.

131

Tales From the Road...

While working as Director of Media Relations for the Florida Association of Realtors® (FAR), I donated a week at my vacation property to FAR's Educational Foundation Auction. I prepared a description of the condo and provided a color photo of the exterior. I included a brochure on Kiawah Island so those unfamiliar with the resort could get a quick overview.

I specified that the successful bidder could select any week they wanted, based on availability. I included the seasonal rental rates so that bidders would know the "street value" of the accommodations.

One of FAR's committee chairmen successfully bid on the prize. His bid was about $100 less than the prevailing rental rate. He got a deal on his vacation. My donated week raised about $600 for the Educational Foundation.

NOTE: You cannot deduct the value of the trip as an expense on your taxes, although you can deduct any actual expenses, such as the utilities for the week, and any clean-up charges billed to you by your management company. For more information, see the article in Section 2 of this book by Valerie Terry of Jackson Hewitt Tax Service, or check with your accountant for further clarification on your own personal situation.

It is one of the most beautiful compensations of life, that no man can sincerely try to help another without helping himself.
— Ralph Waldo Emerson

While this technique will not help your immediate cash flow, you may realize several long-term benefits:

- Every community member who purchases a raffle ticket learns of your property.

- The winner of your prize becomes a living advertisement for your business. The winner may visit your property at his/her expense in future years and refer friends and neighbors.

- You have performed a civic duty to your community by helping to raise funds. You have used your resort property to increase your status in the community, which is truly maximizing your resort property investment.

Action Step:

 Select a community fund-raising project and donate a week's trip to the cause.

 Check with your accountant to report donations on your taxes.

Call Out the Reserves

Many vacation property owners find that each season they have prime weeks that go unused. Their $150,000 beachfront condominium sits vacant in the summer sun. Their $200,000 A-frame on the ski slopes is deserted as thousands of skiers swoosh by. "Even during the peak season at our resort, we always seem to have a few weeks that go unrented," lamented a vacation property owner in North Carolina.

Here's a strategy you can use to fill those vacancies: Call out the reserves! For a vacation property owner, your reserves can be a network of family members, close friends, and business associates. Just like the military reserves, your vacation property owner reserves can be called upon only in an emergency. And an emergency to a vacation property owner is a week during the peak season when their property is not rented.

> *Obstacles are those frightful things you see when you take your eyes off the goal.*
> — Hannah More

The travel industry has long recognized the need to fill last minute vacancies by offering travelers substantial discounts if they fly standby, or fill a bed, or take a cruise on a few days or a few weeks notice.

You can employ this same technique. Develop your list of standbys. Alert them well in advance of their opportunity of a budget vacation at your luxury resort. A vacation at a savings of hundreds of dollars. Then, when you find that you have a week that is going to go unrented, call out the reserves. Call your friends and relatives and book them for that week.

If you discount the rent from, say, $700 to perhaps $500 or even $400 for the week, you are still producing a return on your investment. Also, you have exposed a friend or business associate to your property. They may return. They may refer their friends and business associates to rent your condo.

For your relatives and very close friends, you may want to give them a week or charge them only for the cleanup charges and utilities.

Producing income for your investment is an important objective. By renting to relatives, friends, and business associates at a reduced rate, you are achieving that objective, while you create goodwill and expand your pool of previous and potential renters. With a little thought and planning, you can put those otherwise vacant weeks to good use.

Action Steps:

 Develop a list of reserves.

 Contact them when you realize you have a week you cannot rent.

 Fill that vacant week with a reserve at a discount price.

When You Sell:

Keeping the Dream Alive

There may well come a time when you decide you want or need to sell your vacation property. When that time arrives, remember that timing is everything. The best time to sell a vacation property is just before or during the peak season. You should be able to sell it more quickly and get the highest price possible during this time. If you wait until the off season, your property is likely to be on the market longer and may not bring the best price.

If you're selling, but you're not quite ready to give up the dream entirely, negotiate with the buyer to keep some of the weeks for yourself.

Off the wall? Coming from left field? Have you lost your marbles? Not really.

The more I noodle with this idea, the more I like it. In buying or selling any property, sellers and buyers negotiate many items: price, closing date, closing costs, commissions, furnishings, taxes, etc.

If you are selling a vacation property, negotiate keeping a week or two for yourself for the near future. For example, a prospective buyer might offer you $3000 less than your asking price of $125,000 for your property.

If you can count your money, you don't have a billion dollars.
— J. Paul Getty

You counter with this: "We will accept your offer of $122,000 if you will include one week's free rental at the property to us during the last full week of September for the next 3 years."

In this way, you can keep the dream alive for a little while longer.

Action Steps:

 Sell just before or during peak season.

 Negotiate with the buyer to keep some of the weeks for yourself.

YOU'RE READY TO BUY:

Contact the Coldwell Banker
Resort Property Network™

Directory of Coldwell Banker Resort Property Network™ *Offices*

Coldwell Banker has more than 800 offices that specialize in vacation markets. Sales associates in these offices are skilled and knowledgeable about local property information and about the area amenities that make their market attractive to vacationers.

Coldwell Banker also recognizes that vacation markets generally fall into one of four different geographical types — Mountain; Desert; Lake & Stream; or, Ocean & Shoreline. Some market types may fit into more than one category, i.e., Lake & Stream and Mountain. Recognizing that most vacation customers desire a specific geographical market type, Coldwell Banker has identified each of its Resort Property Network™ offices below with a symbol identifying the type(s) of market they represent. The legend at the bottom of each page identifies the designated symbols. Visit Coldwell Banker Online™ on the Internet at www.coldwellbanker.com for the most up-to-date list of resort market offices and available properties.

Whether you are interested in renting, purchasing or selling a vacation property, the specialists at the Coldwell Banker offices that follow are a valuable resource to consider.

ALASKA

Coldwell Banker
Properties Unlimited Inc.
2801 C Street
Anchorage, AK,USA
(907) 562-2378
M

Coldwell Banker
Whiting Realty
2075 Jordan Avenue
Juneau, AK, USA
(907) 789-0555
MO

Market Type Designations: **M**=Mountain; **D**=Desert;
L=Lake & Stream; **O**=Ocean & Shoreline

ALABAMA

Coldwell Banker
Young Johnston & Associates, Inc.
243 East Barbour Street
Eufaula, AL, USA
(334) 687-2431
L

Coldwell Banker
Charles Hayes Real Estate, Inc.
24190 U.S. Highway 98
Fairhope, AL, USA
(334) 990-6622
O

Coldwell Banker
Graben Real Estate, Inc.
1212 Gunter Avenue
Guntersville, AL, USA
(205) 582-6900
L

Coldwell Banker
Charles Hayes Real Estate, Inc.
1120 Hillcrest Road, #1A
Mobile, AL, USA
(800)741-3928
O

Coldwell Banker
Wedowee Realty
804 W. Broad Street
Wedowee, AL, USA
(205) 357-2215
L

ARKANSAS

Coldwell Banker
Arka-Vista Realty
2770 Bella Vista Way
Bella Vista, AR, USA
(800) 877-6123
ML

Coldwell Banker
Ken Stall & Associates
910 Rogers Ave - Hwy 103 South
Clarksville, AR, USA
(800) 282-8512
ML

Coldwell Banker
Salter Real Estate, Inc.
2850 Prince Street
Conway, AR, USA
(501) 327-6681
M

Coldwell Banker
KC Realty
33 Van Buren Street
Eureka Springs, AR, USA
(501) 253-9161
ML

Coldwell Banker
Faucette Real Estate, Inc.
3589 North College Ave.
Fayetteville, AR, USA
(800) 293-0220
ML

Coldwell Banker
Ozark Real Estate Company
P.O. Box 182, Hwy 62/167/412
Hardy, AR, USA
(870) 856-3206
ML

Coldwell Banker
Homestead Realty Of Harrison, Inc.
1603 Highway 62-65, North
Harrison, AR, USA
(501) 741-2222
ML

Coldwell Banker
Kimble-Bottoms, Inc.
814 Higdon Ferry
Hot Springs, AR, USA
(888) 624-7117
ML

Market Type Designations: **M**=Mountain; **D**=Desert;
L=Lake & Stream; **O**=Ocean & Shoreline

Coldwell Banker
McClure Real Estate
230 South. Olive
Malvern, AR, USA
(501) 332-2777
ML

Coldwell Banker
Colonial Real Estate, Inc.
420 South Main
Mountain Home, AR, USA
(501) 425-6385
ML

ARIZONA

Coldwell Banker
A. I. P.
1137 Highway 95
Bullhead City, AZ, USA
(520) 754-7653
DL

Coldwell Banker
Brothers Realty, Inc.
Box 5785, 36889 Tom Darlington
Carefree, AZ, USA
(602) 488-9595
D

Coldwell Banker
NARICO
1515 E. Cedar Ave, Suite D-1
Flagstaff, AZ, USA
(520) 779-4596
M

Coldwell Banker
Desert Sunrise Realty
17100 E Shea Blvd, Ste. 120
Fountain Hills, AZ, USA
(602) 837-7990
D

Coldwell Banker
The Judd Group, Inc.
3001 Andy Devine Avenue
Kingman, AZ, USA
(520) 718-2001
MDL

Coldwell Banker
The Judd Group, Inc.
65 N. Lake Havasu Ave.
Lake Havasu City, AZ, USA
(520) 855-2191
DL

Coldwell Banker
Success Realty
1212 N. Spencer
Mesa, AZ, USA
(602) 834-9131
D

Coldwell Banker
Success Realty
1148 W. Baseline Road
Mesa, AZ, USA
(602) 839-8200
D

Coldwell Banker
Success Realty
1745 S. Alma School Rd, #145
Mesa, AZ, USA
(602) 730-5200
D

Coldwell Banker
Success Realty
1234 S. Power Rd, #250
Mesa, AZ, USA
(602) 396-7550
D

Coldwell Banker
At Lake Powell
148 6th Ave. Suite 2
Page, AZ, USA
(520) 645-8119
DL

Coldwell Banker
Union Park Real Estate
715 South Beeline Hwy.
Payson, AZ, USA
(520) 474-2216
M

Market Type Designations: **M**=Mountain; **D**=Desert;
L=Lake & Stream; **O**=Ocean & Shoreline

Coldwell Banker
Success Realty
3310 W. Cheryl Dr. #100
Phoenix, AZ, USA
(602) 870-8000
D

Coldwell Banker
Success Realty
4040 E. Camelback #225
Phoenix, AZ, USA
(602) 955-0390
D

Coldwell Banker
Success Realty
2525 E. Camelback Rd, # 150
Phoenix, AZ, USA
(602) 954-6888
D

Coldwell Banker
Success Realty
402 E. Greenway Parkway, #C-28
Phoenix, AZ, USA
(602) 789-1112
D

Coldwell Banker
Brothers Realty, Inc.
23030 North Pima Road
Scottsdale, AZ, USA
(602) 585-0809
D

Coldwell Banker
Success Realty
6929 E.Greenway Pkwy Suite 180
Scottsdale, AZ, USA
(602) 867-2000
D

Coldwell Banker
Success Realty
10605 N. Hayden Rd, #102
Scottsdale, AZ, USA
(602) 951-1010
D

Coldwell Banker
Success Realty
23425 N. Scottsdale Road #9
Scottsdale, AZ, USA
(602) 585-6500
D

Coldwell Banker
Success Realty
6590 N. Scottsdale Rd
Scottsdale, AZ, USA
(602) 991-3300
D

Coldwell Banker
First Affiliate
195 West Highway 89A
Sedona, AZ, USA
(520) 282-4666
MD

Coldwell Banker
McCarty Realty
3191 South White Mountain Road
Show Low, AZ, USA
(520) 537-4321
M

Coldwell Banker
Sun Haven Realty, Inc.
2700 East Fry Blvd. #A-7
Sierra Vista, AZ, USA
(520) 458-3324
D

Coldwell Banker
Success Realty
655 W. Warner Rd., Suite 101
Tempe, AZ, USA
(602) 496-9001
D

Coldwell Banker
Success Realty
5340 E. Broadway
Tucson, AZ, USA
(520) 745-4545
D

Market Type Designations: M=Mountain; D=Desert;
L=Lake & Stream; O=Ocean & Shoreline

Coldwell Banker
Success Realty
5605 E. River Road #219
Tucson, AZ, USA
(520) 577-7433
D

Coldwell Banker
Success Realty
6970 N. Oracle Road #100
Tucson, AZ, USA
(520) 544-4545
D

Coldwell Banker
Bob Nuth & Associates
300 N. Tegner Street
Wickenburg, AZ, USA
(520) 684-2833
D

Coldwell Banker
Town & Country Realty, Inc.
575 E. 32nd Street
Yuma, AZ, USA
(520) 726-5000
D

CALIFORNIA

Coldwell Banker
Sellers Realty
985 G Street
Arcata, CA, USA
(707) 822-5971
MO

Coldwell Banker
Hecker Realty
908 Moran Road
Arnold, CA, USA
(209) 795-1351
M

Coldwell Banker
Camino Real Properties, Inc.
7450 Morro Road
Atascadero, CA, USA
(805) 466-3600
M

Coldwell Banker
Balboa Island
315 Marine Ave.
Balboa Island, CA, USA
(714) 673-6900
O

Coldwell Banker
Mountain Gallery, Realtors
Box 6820, 42153 Big Bear Blvd.
Big Bear Lake, CA, USA
(909) 866-3481
ML

Coldwell Banker
LeeAnn Rasmuson &
Associates, Inc.
370 W. Line St.
Bishop, CA, USA
(760) 873-4264
ML

Coldwell Banker
Coast Properties
Box 100, 555 Highway One
Bodega Bay, CA, USA
(707) 875-2200
O

Coldwell Banker
1st Borrego Springs Properties
Box 951, 569 Palm Canyon Dr.
Borrego Springs, CA, USA
(760) 767-5093
D

Coldwell Banker
Intermountain Realty
37177 Main Street
Burney, CA, USA
(916) 335-3588
M

Coldwell Banker
Don Bricker Real Estate, Inc.
702 Main Street
Cambria, CA, USA
(805) 927-3834
O

Market Type Designations: **M**=Mountain; **D**=Desert;
L=Lake & Stream; **O**=Ocean & Shoreline

Coldwell Banker
Associated Brokers Realty
31620 Railroad Canyon Road
Canyon Lake, CA, USA
(909) 244-1867
L

Coldwell Banker
Dana Pt./San Clemente
27111 Camino De Estrella
Capistrano Beach, CA, USA
(714) 661-9355
O

Coldwell Banker
Carlsbad
5050 Avenida Encinas Ste. #160
Carlsbad, CA, USA
(760) 438-2922
O

Coldwell Banker
Del Monte Realty -
Carmel By The Sea
P.O. BOX 350
Carmel, CA, USA
(800) 464-4292
MO

Coldwell Banker
Del Monte Realty -
Carmel Rancho
26611 Carmel Center Place
Carmel, CA, USA
(800) 464-4292
MO

Coldwell Banker
Liberty Realty
48 Ocean Avenue
Cayucos, CA, USA
(805) 995-3505
O

Coldwell Banker
Kehr/O'Brien Real Estate
Box 556, 244 Main St.
Chester, CA, USA
(530) 258-2103
ML

Coldwell Banker
Newport Beach
2121 East Coast Hwy. Suite 180
Corona Del Mar, CA, USA
(714) 644-9060
O

Coldwell Banker
Coronado
1340 Orange Avenue
Coronado, CA, USA
(619) 437-1853
O

Coldwell Banker
Rim O' The World Realty
PO Box 689, 24028 Lake Dr.
Crestline, CA, USA
(909) 338-1763
M

Coldwell Banker
Del Mar
2651 Via De La Valle
Del Mar, CA, USA
(619) 755-0075
O

Coldwell Banker
Amaral & Associates, Realtors
1520 Discovery Bay Blvd.
Discovery Bay, CA, USA
(925) 634-0400
O

Coldwell Banker
Exceptional Properties
3941 Park Dr., Suite 80
El Dorado Hills, CA, USA
(916) 933-2444
M

Coldwell Banker
J. Heaton & Associates
508 N. Kaweah
Exeter, CA, USA
(209) 592-5192
M

Market Type Designations: **M**=Mountain; **D**=Desert;
L=Lake & Stream; **O**=Ocean & Shoreline

Coldwell Banker
Six Rivers Real Estate
910 S. Fortuna Blvd.
Fortuna, CA, USA
(707) 725-9376
M

Coldwell Banker
Mountain Leisure Properties
Box 848, 18687 Main Street
Groveland, CA, USA
(209) 962-5252
ML

Coldwell Banker
Pacific Real Estate
39351 South Highway One
Gualala, CA, USA
(707) 884-3866
O

Coldwell Banker
Half Moon Bay
40 N.Cabrillo Hwy.
Half Moon Bay, CA, USA
(800) 464-4292
O

Coldwell Banker
Wright Realty
610 E. Florida Ave., Suite A
Hemet, CA, USA
(909) 658-2149
D

Coldwell Banker
Sandpiper Realty
45000 Club Drive
Indian Wells, CA, USA
(760) 345-2527
D

Coldwell Banker
Award-Realtors, Inc.
106 Water Street
Jackson, CA, USA
(209) 223-2276
ML

Coldwell Banker
1st June Lake Properties
Box 238 Lodge A Boulder Drive
June Lake, CA, USA
(760) 648-7505
ML

Coldwell Banker
La Jolla
930 Prospect Street
La Jolla, CA, USA
(619) 459-3851
O

Coldwell Banker
Laguna Beach
660 N. Coastal Highway
Laguna Beach, CA, USA
(714) 494-0215
O

Coldwell Banker
Laguna Beach South
31601 Pacific Coast Hwy
Laguna Beach, CA, USA
(714) 499-1320
O

Coldwell Banker
Sky Ridge Realty
Box 1089, 28200 State Hwy. 189
Lake Arrowhead, CA, USA
(909) 336-2131
ML

Coldwell Banker
Towne And Country
190 S. Main
Lakeport, CA, USA
(707) 262-1000
L

Coldwell Banker
CoastCo Real Estate
5550 E. 7th Street
Long Beach, CA, USA
(562) 498-6501
O

Market Type Designations: **M**=Mountain; **D**=Desert;
L=Lake & Stream; **O**=Ocean & Shoreline

Coldwell Banker
Leisure Real Estate
3293 Main St
Mammoth Lakes, CA, USA
(800) 266-6966
ML

Coldwell Banker
Mother Lode Properties, Inc.
P.O. Box 1129, 5108 Hwy. 140
Mariposa, CA, USA
(209) 742-7000
M

Coldwell Banker
Jon Douglas - Montecito
1290 Coast Village Road
Montecito, CA, USA
(805) 969-4755
O

Coldwell Banker
Liberty Realty
798 Morro Bay Blvd.
Morro Bay, CA, USA
(805) 772-4447
O

Coldwell Banker
Mountain Gate Properties
426 N. Mt. Shasta Blvd.
Mount Shasta, CA, USA
(916) 926-5236
ML

Coldwell Banker
Dan Blough & Associates
40050 Hwy 49, Suite 10
Oakhurst, CA, USA
(209) 642-2100
ML

Coldwell Banker
Property Shoppe
727 W. Ojai Ave.
Ojai, CA, USA
(805) 646-7288
M

Coldwell Banker
Eadie Adams Realty
501 S. Indian Canyon
Palm Springs, CA, USA
(760) 778-5500
D

Coldwell Banker
Palos Verdes Peninsula Center
430 Silver Spur Road
Palos Verdes, CA, USA
(310)541-2421
O

Coldwell Banker
Ponderosa Real Estate, Inc.
7020 Skyway
Paradise, CA, USA
(916) 877-6244
M

Coldwell Banker
Del Monte Realty - Pebble Beach
17 Mile Drive at Palmero
Pebble Beach, CA, USA
(800) 464-4292
O

Coldwell Banker
Foothill Realty
P.O. Box 290459
Phelan, CA, USA
(619) 949-4414
D

Coldwell Banker
Award-Realtors, Inc.
26582 Highway 88
Pioneer, CA, USA
(209) 295-3800
M

Coldwell Banker
Dan Blough & Associates
880 Price Street
Pismo Beach, CA, USA
(805) 773-6611
O

Market Type Designations: **M**=Mountain; **D**=Desert;
L=Lake & Stream; **O**=Ocean & Shoreline

Coldwell Banker
Gerwer & Associates, Inc.
111 Main Street
Placerville, CA, USA
(530) 626-3333
M

Coldwell Banker
Pioneer Realty
372 W. Main Street
Quincy, CA, USA
(530) 283-0370
B

Coldwell Banker
Rancho Santa Fe
6015 Paseo Delicias P.O. 2225
Rancho Santa Fe, CA, USA
(619) 756-4481
O

Coldwell Banker
C & C Properties
2120 Churn Creek Rd., Suite A
Redding, CA, USA
(530) 221-7550
L

Coldwell Banker
First Shasta Realty
2837 Bechelli Lane
Redding, CA, USA
(916) 221-0111
L

Coldwell Banker
Source One Realty
2502 Artesia Blvd.
Redondo Beach, CA, USA
(310) 798-8700
O

Coldwell Banker
The Running Springs Realty
Box 1711, 31980 Hilltop Blvd.
Running Springs, CA, USA
(909) 867-7001
M

Coldwell Banker
Pacific Beach
4090 Mission Blvd.
San Diego, CA, USA
(619) 488-4090
O

Coldwell Banker
Point Loma
2727 Shelter Island Drive
San Diego, CA, USA
(619) 224-5111
O

Coldwell Banker
Jon Douglas Company - Santa
Barbara
3902 State Street
Santa Barbara, CA, USA
(805) 563-7200
O

Coldwell Banker
Premier Properties
1515 Chapala Street
Santa Barbara, CA, USA
(805) 963-7587
O

Coldwell Banker
Premier Properties
1111 Coast Village Road
Santa Barbara, CA, USA
(805) 969-7810
O

Coldwell Banker
Dan Blough & Associates
2400 Professional Pkwy., #100
Santa Maria, CA, USA
(805) 934-1000
O

Coldwell Banker
Sausalito
3 Harbor Drive - Ste. 100
Sausalito, CA, USA
(800) 464-4292
MO

Market Type Designations: **M**=Mountain; **D**=Desert;
L=Lake & Stream; **O**=Ocean & Shoreline

Coldwell Banker
Shaver Lake Real Estate, Inc.
Box 349, 41593 Tollhouse Road
Shaver Lake, CA, USA
(800) 879-8989
ML

Coldwell Banker
Premier Properties
1607 Mission Drive, Suite A
Solvang, CA, USA
(805) 688-7098
L

Coldwell Banker
Mother Lode Real Estate
13854 Mono Way
Sonora, CA, USA
(209) 532-6993
ML

Coldwell Banker
McKinney & Assoc., Inc., Realtors
2196 Lake Tahoe Blvd.
South Lake Tahoe, CA, USA
(530) 542-5555
ML

Coldwell Banker
Heard Realty
1604 Main Street
Susanville, CA, USA
(916) 257-7113
ML

Coldwell Banker
Hauserman Real Estate
Box 1901, 475 N. Lake Blvd.
Tahoe City, CA, USA
(800) 30-TAHOE
ML

Coldwell Banker
Best Realty
101 E. Tehachapi Blvd.
Tehachapi, CA, USA
(805) 822-5553
M

Coldwell Banker
Trinidad Realty
361 Main Street, PO Box 754
Trinidad, CA, USA
(707) 677-0213
ML

Coldwell Banker
Fraser & Fraser Real Estate
34 Commercial Row
Truckee, CA, USA
(800) 850-2555
ML

Coldwell Banker
Twain Harte Realty
Box 190, 23003 Joaquin Gully
Twain Harte, CA, USA
(209) 586-5200
ML

Coldwell Banker
At Trinity Alps Realty
Box 1390, 1247 Main St.
Weaverville, CA, USA
(916) 623-5581
ML

Coldwell Banker
Bear Creek Properties
32395-B Clinton Keith Road #14
Wildomar, CA, USA
(909) 609-1212
L

Coldwell Banker
Chris Kutzkey, Realtors
1288 S. Main, Suite 5
Yreka, CA, USA
(916) 842-7319
ML

COLORADO

Coldwell Banker
The Aspen Brokers, Ltd.
720 E. Durant Avenue
Aspen, CO, USA
(970) 925-6750
M

Market Type Designations: **M**=Mountain; **D**=Desert;
L=Lake & Stream; **O**=Ocean & Shoreline

Coldwell Banker
Bunchman Real Estate
Box 1598, 137 South Main St.
Breckenridge, CO, USA
(800) 669-5356
M

Coldwell Banker
Bev Coggins Realty
Box 1170, 317 E. Main Street
Buena Vista, CO, USA
(719) 395-6661
M

Coldwell Banker
Walker & Co.
3604 Galley Road
Colorado Springs, CO, USA
(719) 596-7882
M

Coldwell Banker
Bighorn Realty
Box 100, 311 6th Street
Crested Butte, CO, USA
(970) 349-5313
M

Coldwell Banker
Colorado Rockies Real Estate
Box 1666, 135 Main Street
Dillon, CO, USA
(970) 468-9300
M

Coldwell Banker
Heritage House, Realtors
785 Main Ave.
Durango, CO, USA
(970) 259-3333
M

Coldwell Banker
Estes Village Properties, Ltd.
320 East Elkhorn Ave, Box 4130
Estes Park, CO, USA
(970) 586-4425
M

Coldwell Banker
Colorado Rockies Real Estate
619 Main Street, Suite 7
Frisco, CO, USA
(970) 668-0900
M

Coldwell Banker
Buzick & Assoc., LLC
901 Grand Ave., Suite B
Glenwood Springs, CO, USA
(970) 945-6000
M

Coldwell Banker
The Pagosa Group
2383 Highway 160 West
Pagosa Springs, CO, USA
(970) 731-2000
M

Coldwell Banker
Mountain Realty
157 US Highway 550 P O Box 398
Ridgway, CO, USA
(970) 626-5455
M

Coldwell Banker
Silver Oak, Ltd.
200 Lincoln Avenue Box 775023
Steamboat Springs, CO, USA
(970) 879-8814
M

Coldwell Banker
Shaw & Company, Inc.
220 W. Colorado - P.O. Box 670
Telluride, CO, USA
(970) 728-4466
M

Coldwell Banker
Big Pine Realty
227 North Commercial Street
Trinidad, CO, USA
(719) 846-2291
M

Market Type Designations: M=Mountain; D=Desert;
L=Lake & Stream; O=Ocean & Shoreline

Coldwell Banker
Timberline Real Estate, Inc.
286 Bridge Street
Vail, CO, USA
(970) 476-2113
M

Coldwell Banker
Saffell
Box 92,111 Cooper Creek Sq, Hw
Winter Park, CO, USA
(970) 726-8831
M

Coldwell Banker
1st Choice Realty, Inc.
400 W. Midland Ave
Woodland Park, CO, USA
(719) 687-0900
M

CONNECTICUT

Coldwell Banker
Browning & Browning Real
Estate, LLC
240 Providence Rd
Brooklyn, CT, USA
(800) 321-6791
O

Coldwell Banker
Darien
870 Post Road
Darien, CT, USA
(203) 655-0208
O

Coldwell Banker
Chelsey Realty
15 Main Street PO Box 286
East Haddam, CT, USA
(860) 873-1401
O

Coldwell Banker
Coast & Country Real Estate
432 Main Street
East Haven, CT, USA
(203) 466-0000
O

Coldwell Banker
Leighton Realty
1663 Route 12
Gales Ferry, CT, USA
(860) 464-7231
O

Coldwell Banker
Greenwich
32 Field Point Road
Greenwich, CT, USA
(203) 622-1100
O

Coldwell Banker
Yankee Realty
24 Washington Avenue
North Haven, CT, USA
(203) 239-2553
O

Coldwell Banker
Norwalk
185 East Ave.
Norwalk, CT, USA
(203) 853-6601
O

Coldwell Banker
J H & H, Inc., Realtors
30 Westbrook Place
Westbrook, CT, USA
(860) 399-7202
O

Coldwell Banker
Westport
305 Post Road East
Westport, CT, USA
(203) 227-1269
O

DELAWARE

Coldwell Banker
Rehoboth Resort Realty
800 Kings Highway
Lewes, DE, USA
(302) 645-2881
L

Market Type Designations: M=Mountain; D=Desert;
L=Lake & Stream; O=Ocean & Shoreline

Coldwell Banker
Rehoboth Resort Realty
4157 Highway One
Rehoboth Beach, DE, USA
(302) 227-5000
O

Coldwell Banker
Broadcreek Realty
P.O. Box 598 Route 13
Seaford, DE, USA
(800) 221-5575
O

FLORIDA

Coldwell Banker
Anna Maria/Bradenton
605-C Manatee Avenue West
Anna Maria Island, FL, USA
(800) 624-5292
O

Coldwell Banker
Dolphin Realty
202 Apollo Beach Blvd.
Apollo Beach, FL, USA
(813) 645-8495
O

Coldwell Banker
Belleair/Clearwater
2811 West Bay Drive
Belleair Bluffs, FL, USA
(800) 624-5292
O

Coldwell Banker
Schmitt Real Estate Co.
30646 Overseas Hwy-POB 430079
Big Pine Key, FL, USA
(305) 872-3050
O

Coldwell Banker
Boca Centre
101 N. Federal Highway
Boca Raton, FL, USA
(561) 391-9097
O

Coldwell Banker
Boynton Beach/Delray
3301 West Boynton Beach Blvd
Boynton Beach, FL, USA
(561) 734-3338
O

Coldwell Banker
El Conquistador/Bradenton
3403 El Conquistador Parkway
Bradenton, FL, USA
(800) 624-5292
O

Coldwell Banker
Manatee Avenue/Bradenton
6302 Manatee Avenue West
Bradenton, FL, USA
(800) 624-5292
O

Coldwell Banker
Bloomingdale/Brandon
889 E. Bloomingdale Blvd.
Brandon, FL, USA
(800) 624-5292
O

Coldwell Banker
Brandon/Tampa
777 West Lumsden Road
Brandon, FL, USA
(800) 624-5292
O

Coldwell Banker
Central Brandon
1755 Brandon Blvd.
Brandon, FL, USA
(800) 624-5292
O

Coldwell Banker
McFadden & Sprowls
3301 Del Prado Blvd
Cape Coral, FL, USA
(941) 945-1414
O

Market Type Designations: M=Mountain; D=Desert;
L=Lake & Stream; O=Ocean & Shoreline

Coldwell Banker
Clearwater
1724 Gulf to Bay Blvd
Clearwater, FL, USA
(800) 624-5292
O

Coldwell Banker
Countryside/Clearwater
2536 Countryside Blvd
Clearwater, FL, USA
(800) 624-5292
O

Coldwell Banker
Trafford Realty Co.
305 Brevard Avenue
Cocoa, FL, USA
(407) 636-3131
O

Coldwell Banker
1st U.S. Area Realty, Inc.
1 South Orlando Ave.
Cocoa Beach, FL, USA
(407) 784-5796
O

Coldwell Banker
Coconut Grove
2960 Oak Avenue
Coconut Grove, FL, USA
(305) 445-1700
O

Coldwell Banker
McGeehan & Sons
1100 SE Highway 19, Suite 200
Crystal River, FL, USA
(352) 795-3602
O

Coldwell Banker
Besst Realty Inc.
2429 N. Atlantic Ave. #39
Daytona Beach, FL, USA
(904) 672-2200
O

Coldwell Banker
Major League Realty, Inc.
1625 Taylor Rd
Daytona Beach, FL, USA
(800) 752-5021
O

Coldwell Banker
Major League Realty, Inc.
3300 South Atlantic Ave.
Daytona Beach, FL, USA
(800) 749-1234
O

Coldwell Banker
All Star Real Estate Services
737 Highway 98 East, Suite #2
Destin, FL, USA
(850) 837-5523
O

Coldwell Banker
Sunstar Realty, Inc.
1951 S. McCall Rd., #625
Englewood, FL, USA
(941) 475-0009
O

Coldwell Banker
McFadden & Sprowls
7500 College Parkway
Fort Myers, FL, USA
(941) 939-3336
O

Coldwell Banker
Ft Lauderdale Northeast
2495 E. Commerical Blvd
Ft. Lauderdale, FL, USA
(954) 491-0700
O

Coldwell Banker
Ft Lauderdale Southeast
1306 SE 17 St. Causeway
Ft. Lauderdale, FL, USA
(954) 523-8440
O

Market Type Designations: M=Mountain; D=Desert;
L=Lake & Stream; O=Ocean & Shoreline

Coldwell Banker
Ft Lauderdale/Sea Ranch
4727 N. Ocean Blvd
Ft. Lauderdale, FL, USA
(954) 781-9393
O

Coldwell Banker
Preferred Properties
4935 Sheridan Street
Hollywood, FL, USA
(954) 987-1140
O

Coldwell Banker
Sun Land Realty Of Florida, Inc.
1918 Highway A1A
Indian Harbor Beach, FL, USA
(407) 773-1480
O

Coldwell Banker
Investors Realty Of
Citrus County, Inc.
314 West Main Street
Inverness, FL, USA
(800) 877-9533
L

Coldwell Banker
Walter Williams Realty, Inc.
10450 San Jose Blvd.
Jacksonville, FL, USA
(904) 268-3000
O

Coldwell Banker
Walter Williams Realty, Inc.
10450 San Jose Blvd.
Jacksonville, FL, USA
(904) 262-2442
O

Coldwell Banker
Jupiter
17380 Alternate A-1-A
Jupiter, FL, USA
(561) 748-5900
LO

Coldwell Banker
Key Biscayne
328 Crandon Blvd, Suite 127
Key Biscayne, FL, USA
(305) 361 5722
O

Coldwell Banker
Schmitt Real Estate Co.
2720-A N. Roosevelt Blvd.
Key West, FL, USA
(305) 296-7727
O

Coldwell Banker
Solomon Real Estate Group, Inc.
851 Buenaventura Blvd
Kissimmee, FL, USA
(407) 348-3322
L

Coldwell Banker
Lake Mary/Orlando
3801 W. Lake Mary Blvd., #123
Lake Mary, FL, USA
(800) 624-5292
L

Coldwell Banker
Stephen L. Miller Realty
2203 US 27 North
Lake Placid, FL, USA
(800) 356-7397
L

Coldwell Banker
Advantage Team Realty
3948 Lake Padgett Drive
Land O` Lakes, FL, USA
(813) 996-4747
LO

Coldwell Banker
Longboat Key
201 Gulf of Mexico Drive
Longboat Key, FL, USA
(800) 624-5292
O

Market Type Designations: **M**=Mountain; **D**=Desert;
L=Lake & Stream; **O**=Ocean & Shoreline

Coldwell Banker
St Armands/Sarasota
423 St. Armands Circle
Longboat Key, FL, USA
(800) 624-5292
O

Coldwell Banker
Longwood/Orlando
2160 W. Highway 434, #100
Longwood, FL, USA
(800) 624-5292
L

Coldwell Banker
Schmitt Real Estate Co.
11100 Overseas Highway
Marathon, FL, USA
(800) 366-5181
O

Coldwell Banker
McFadden & Sprowls
928 N. Collier Blvd.
Marco Island, FL, USA
(941) 394-8121
O

Coldwell Banker
Simmons Realty
2867 Caledonia Street
Marianna, FL, USA
(904) 526-4663
O

Coldwell Banker
Miami Beach / N.E. Miami
1440 J. F. K. Causeway - #100
Miami Beach, FL, USA
(305) 867-2300
O

Coldwell Banker
McFadden & Sprowls
3701 Tamiami Trail North
Naples, FL, USA
(941) 261-1551
O

Coldwell Banker
Standel Realty
8825 Navarre Parkway
Navarre, FL, USA
(904) 939-5232
O

Coldwell Banker
F.I. Grey & Son, Inc. Realtor
6328 US Highway 19
New Port Richey, FL, USA
(813) 849-2424
O

Coldwell Banker
New Port Richey
4309 US Hwy 19
New Port Richey, FL, USA
(800) 624-5292
O

Coldwell Banker
Suncoast Realty
4780 US 19 North
New Port Richey, FL, USA
(813) 848-3222
O

Coldwell Banker
Major League Realty, Inc.
176 Corbin Park Rd
New Smyrna Beach, FL, USA
(800) 752-5021
O

Coldwell Banker
Berger Real Estate
800 South Parrott Avenue
Okeechobee, FL, USA
(941) 763-5335
L

Coldwell Banker
Southeast Orlando
4446 Curry Ford Road
Orlando, FL, USA
(407) 306-8787
L

Market Type Designations: M=Mountain; D=Desert;
L=Lake & Stream; O=Ocean & Shoreline

Coldwell Banker
Southwest Orlando
7347 Sandlake Road
Orlando, FL, USA
(407) 352-1040
L

Coldwell Banker
Oviedo/Orlando
1419 W. Broadway
Oviedo, FL, USA
(800) 624-5292
L

Coldwell Banker
Heiser Realty, Inc.
39 Old Kings Road North
Palm Coast, FL, USA
(904) 445-5880
O

Coldwell Banker
Palm Harbor/Clearwater
3217 Tampa Road
Palm Harbor, FL, USA
(800) 624-5292
O

Coldwell Banker
Carroll Realty, Inc.
2551 Jenks Avenue
Panama City, FL, USA
(904) 872-8200
O

Coldwell Banker
Walter Williams Realty, Inc.
110 Solano Road
Ponte Vedra Beach, FL, USA
(904) 285-8800
O

Coldwell Banker
Sunstar Realty, Inc.
1951-D Tamiami Trail
Port Charlotte, FL, USA
(941) 629-1245
O

Coldwell Banker
B & B Properties of
Gulf County, Inc.
8022 Cape San Blas Road
Port St. Joe, FL, USA
(850) 227-1892
O

Coldwell Banker
Success Realty, Inc.
9580 S Federal Highway
Port St. Lucie, FL, USA
(561) 337-1177
O

Coldwell Banker
Morris Realty, Inc.
2825 Tamiami Trail
Punta Gorda, FL, USA
(813) 637-1090
O

Coldwell Banker
Redington/St. Petersburg
17635 Gulf Boulevard
Redington Shores, FL, USA
(800) 624-5292
O

Coldwell Banker
Suncoast Realty
224 Franklin Blvd
Saint George Island, FL, USA
(850) 927-2282
O

Coldwell Banker
Tamiami Trail/Sarasota
3100 South Tamiami Trail
Sarasota, FL, USA
(800) 624-5292
O

Coldwell Banker
University/Sarasota
6260 N. Lockwood Ridge Road
Sarasota, FL, USA
(800) 624-5292
O

Market Type Designations: **M**=Mountain; **D**=Desert;
L=Lake & Stream; **O**=Ocean & Shoreline

Coldwell Banker
Siesta Key/Sarasota
5145 Ocean Boulevard
Siesta Key, FL, USA
(800) 624-5292
O

Coldwell Banker
Westshore/Tampa
144A South West Shore Blvd
South Tampa, FL, USA
(800) 624-5292
O

Coldwell Banker
McGeehan & Sons
5426 Spring Hill Drive
Spring Hill, FL, USA
(352) 686-1234
O

Coldwell Banker
Palazzo Realty, Inc.
4085 A1A South
St. Augustine, FL, USA
(904) 471-7661
O

Coldwell Banker
St. Pete Beach/St. Petersburg
6395 Gulf Boulevard
St. Pete Beach, FL, USA
(800) 624-5292
O

Coldwell Banker
Hashem Realty
2201 4th Street North, Suite A
St. Petersburg, FL, USA
(813) 822-8686
O

Coldwell Banker
St. Petersburg Central
3325 66th Street North
St. Petersburgh, FL, USA
(800) 624-5292
O

Coldwell Banker
Hyde Park/Tampa
901 Swann Ave.
Tampa, FL, USA
(800) 624-5292
O

Coldwell Banker
Keys Country Realty
91910 US 1
Tavernier, FL, USA
(305) 852-5254
LO

Coldwell Banker
Treasure Island/St. Petersburg
157 107th Avenue North
Treasure Island, FL, USA
(800) 624-5292
O

Coldwell Banker
Venice
400 Barcelona Avenue
Venice, FL, USA
(800) 624-5292
O

Coldwell Banker
Ed Schlitt, Inc., Realtors
321 21st Street 2d
Vero Beach, FL, USA
(561) 567-1181
O

Coldwell Banker
West Palm Beach Intracoastal
4800 S. Dixie Hwy.
West Palm Beach, FL, USA
(561) 832-4663
O

Coldwell Banker
Winter Park/Orlando
170 West Fairbanks
Winter Park, FL, USA
(800) 624-5292
L

Market Type Designations: M=Mountain; D=Desert;
L=Lake & Stream; O=Ocean & Shoreline

Coldwell Banker
Northeast Orlando
5965 Red Bug Lake Rd., St. 101
Winter Springs, FL, USA
(800) 624-5292
L

GEORGIA

Coldwell Banker
Tate Realty, Inc.
167 Big Canoe
Big Canoe, GA, USA
(770) 893-3333
ML

Coldwell Banker
Birdie White Realty
680 Gainesville Hwy
Blairsville, GA, USA
(706) 745-2473
M

Coldwell Banker
High Country Realty
Hwy 5 North Jones Bldg Box295
Blue Ridge, GA, USA
(706) 632-7311
ML

Coldwell Banker
Seckinger Realty Company
3355 Cypress Mill Road
Brunswick, GA, USA
(912) 264-9050
O

Coldwell Banker
North Metro Realty
4690 South Lee Street
Buford, GA, USA
(770) 945-6736
L

Coldwell Banker
Hal West Realty
US Hwy 441 So., P.O.Box 1234
Clayton, GA, USA
(706) 782-2222
ML

Coldwell Banker
French Properties, Inc.
889 Buford Road
Cumming, GA, USA
(770) 889-4080
L

Coldwell Banker
Dahlonega Realty, Inc.
100 Schultz Ave.
Dahlonega, GA, USA
(706) 864-3142
M

Coldwell Banker
French Properties
Hwy. 400 & Hwy. 53
Dawsonville, GA, USA
(706) 216-7000
L

Coldwell Banker
Heritage Real Estate
501 Candler Street
Gainesville, GA, USA
(770) 536-9700
L

Coldwell Banker
Lake Oconee Realty
2001 Linger Longer Road
Greensboro, GA, USA
(706) 467-3181
L

Coldwell Banker
Coastal Georgia Properties
10384 Ford Avenue PO Box 1269
Richmond Hill, GA, USA
(800) 841-7010
O

Coldwell Banker
Garvin, Realtors
8400 Abercorn Street
Savannah, GA, USA
(912) 925-7777
O

Market Type Designations: M=Mountain; D=Desert;
L=Lake & Stream; O=Ocean & Shoreline

Coldwell Banker
Greater Savannah Realty
1 Diamond Causeway, Suite 10
Savannah, GA, USA
(912) 352-9914
O

Coldwell Banker
Greater Savannah Realty
6349 Abercorn Street
Savannah, GA, USA
(912) 352-1222
O

Coldwell Banker
Greater Savannah Realty
18 East Oglethorpe Avenue
Savannah, GA, USA
(912) 232-7127
O

Coldwell Banker
Towne And Country Realty
1191 Charlie Smith Sr. Highway
St. Marys, GA, USA
(912) 882-3500
O

HAWAII

Coldwell Banker
Pacific Properties
98-211 Pali Momi St.
Aiea, HI, USA
(808) 488-1991
O

Coldwell Banker
DAY-LUM Properties
2 Kamehameha Avenue
Hilo, HI, USA
(808) 935-0399
O

Coldwell Banker
Pacific Properties
1909 Ala Wai Blvd. #C2
Honolulu, HI, USA
(808) 944-1888
O

Coldwell Banker
Pacific Properties
1177 Kapiolani Blvd.
Honolulu, HI, USA
(808) 596-0456
O

Coldwell Banker
Pacific Properties
Kahala Mall Office Ctr, #104
Honolulu, HI, USA
(808) 732-1414
O

Coldwell Banker
Pacific Properties
629 Kailua Rd. #212
Kailua, HI, USA
(808) 261-3314
O

Coldwell Banker
Aloha Properties
75-170 Hualalai Rd, Ste B-105
Kailua-Kona, HI, USA
(808) 329-3545
O

Coldwell Banker
Island Properties
2463 South Kihei Road
Kihei, HI, USA
(808) 879-5233
O

IOWA

Coldwell Banker
Howell Realty, Inc.
309 North 13th Street
Centerville, IA, USA
(515) 437-4700
L

Coldwell Banker
Dominic Goodmann
Real Estate, Ltd.
2774 University, Box 1088
Dubuque, IA, USA
(319) 556-3843
O

Market Type Designations: M=Mountain; D=Desert;
L=Lake & Stream; O=Ocean & Shoreline

Coldwell Banker
Real Estate Professionals
44 Sturgis Corner Dr.
Iowa City, IA, USA
(319) 351-3355
L

Coldwell Banker
Clover Ridge Realtors
5002 Karen Drive Unit 301
Panora, IA, USA
(515) 755-4057
L

IDAHO

Coldwell Banker
Schneidmiller Realty
1924 Northwest Blvd.
Coeur d`Alene, ID, USA
(800) 829-2555
L

Coldwell Banker
The Real Estate Co.
47 S. Main ~ PO Box 174
Driggs, ID, USA
(208) 354-2337
M

Coldwell Banker
Eagle Rock
576 3rd Street
Idaho Falls, ID, USA
(208) 529-4663
M

Coldwell Banker
The Sun Valley Real Estate
Company
Box 515, 471 Leadville Ave., N
Ketchum, ID, USA
(208) 726-4100
M

Coldwell Banker
Johnson & Co.
P.O. Box 1678
Mc Call, ID, USA
(208) 634-8500
ML

Coldwell Banker
Landmark
Box 2559, 920 Deon Dr., Suite
Pocatello, ID, USA
(208) 232-9010
ML

Coldwell Banker
Resort Realty
202 South First Avenue
Sandpoint, ID, USA
(800) 544-1855
ML

Coldwell Banker
Western Realty
590 Addison Avenue
Twin Falls, ID, USA
(800) 743-5927
L

ILLINOIS

Coldwell Banker
Home Trust Realtors
438 Lake Street
Antioch, IL, USA
(847) 395-7575
LO

Coldwell Banker
Havens Inc., Realtors
706 West Main Street
Carbondale, IL, USA
(800) 455-6580
LO

Coldwell Banker
Excel
330 Virginia St
Crystal Lake, IL, USA
(815) 459-5900
L

Coldwell Banker
Schafer, Realtors
406 Keller Drive, Rt. 32 North
Effingham, IL, USA
(217) 347-5123
L

Market Type Designations: **M**=Mountain; **D**=Desert;
L=Lake & Stream; **O**=Ocean & Shoreline

Coldwell Banker
Great American
125-2 E. State Rd.
Island Lake, IL, USA
(847) 526-0001
L

Coldwell Banker
Great American
500 S. Rand Rd.
Lake Zurich, IL, USA
(847) 438-9300
L

Coldwell Banker
1st American
2521 Ridge Road
Lansing, IL, USA
(708) 895-1000
LO

Coldwell Banker
Libertyville
307 S. Milwaukee Road
Libertyville, IL, USA
(800) 827-2836
L

Coldwell Banker
J. David Thompson, Realty
104 South Carbon Street
Marion, IL, USA
(618) 997-1868
LO

Coldwell Banker
Primus Realty
4104 W. Elm Street
McHenry, IL, USA
(815) 385-6990
L

Coldwell Banker
Haeberle & Associates
1715 N. Division
Morris, IL, USA
(815) 942-2705
O

Coldwell Banker
Haeberle & Associates
130 W. Lafayette St.
Ottawa, IL, USA
(815) 434-3337
O

Coldwell Banker
Primus Realty
109 W. Church Street
Sandwich, IL, USA
(815) 786-2100
L

Coldwell Banker
Vernon Hills
270 Hawthorn Village Commons
Vernon Hills, IL, USA
(800) 827-2836
L

Coldwell Banker
Primus Realty
7314 Hancock Drive
Wonder Lake, IL, USA
(815) 653-2061
L

INDIANA

Coldwell Banker
Graber, Realtors
300 N. Wayne St.
Angola, IN, USA
(219) 665-3171
L

Coldwell Banker
American Heritage Realty, Inc.
603 West 30th Street
Connersville, IN, USA
(765) 825-1103
L

Coldwell Banker
Banks Mallough
2777 Maplecrest Road
Ft. Wayne, IN, USA
(219) 486-1956
L

Market Type Designations: M=Mountain; D=Desert;
L=Lake & Stream; O=Ocean & Shoreline

Coldwell Banker
Graber, Realtors
1206 E. Dupont Rd.
Ft. Wayne, IN, USA
(219) 489-3336
L

Coldwell Banker
Crowe-Kissel Realty
766 W. Main St.
Greensburg, IN, USA
(812) 663-4663
L

Coldwell Banker
Lukemeyer Realty, Inc.
310 West 6th Streett
Jasper, IN, USA
(812) 482-2662
L

Coldwell Banker
Schrock Real Estate
716 N. Detroit St.
La Grange, IN, USA
(219) 463-7178
L

Coldwell Banker
Anchor Real Estate
1807 South Bend Ave.
South Bend, IN, USA
(800) 733-0046
L

Coldwell Banker
Leiter Real Estate, Inc.
101 Argonne Road
Warsaw, IN, USA
(219) 267-5955
L

KENTUCKY

Coldwell Banker
Service 1st Realty
110 Merchant St.
Cadiz, KY, USA
(502) 522-4699
L

Coldwell Banker
V.I.P. Realty, Inc.
317 West Main Street
Danville, KY, USA
(606) 236-5450
L

Coldwell Banker
Marshall Realty
3908 Hinkleville
Paducah, KY, USA
(502) 444-6008
L

Coldwell Banker
Bob Johnson Realty, Inc.
111 D West Hwy. 80
Somerset, KY, USA
(606) 678-3032
L

LOUISIANA

Coldwell Banker
White Real Estate
5401 Jackson St Extension
Alexandria, LA, USA
(318) 445-2500
LO

Coldwell Banker
Reinauer Real Estate
409 Iris Street
Lake Charles, LA, USA
(318) 433-4663
LO

Coldwell Banker
Fertitta-Morrow Real Estate
1400 South Fifth Street
Leesville, LA, USA
(318) 239-2626
LO

MASSACHUSETTS

Coldwell Banker
Martha Murray Real Estate
63 Lower County Rd.
Dennisport, MA, USA
(508) 394-2114
O

Market Type Designations: M=Mountain; D=Desert;
L=Lake & Stream; O=Ocean & Shoreline

Coldwell Banker
Linda R. Bassett Real Estate
201 Upper Main St, Box 2222
Edgartown, MA, USA
(508) 627-9201
O

Coldwell Banker
Hayes Associates
150 Front Street
Marion, MA, USA
(508) 748-3044
O

Coldwell Banker
South Shore, Inc.
1297 Ocean Street
Marshfield, MA, USA
(617) 837-2832
O

Coldwell Banker
Atlantic Realty
32 Main Street- P.O. Box 1630
Orleans, MA, USA
(508) 255-8011
O

Coldwell Banker
Willow Realty
2 Willow Street
Sandwich, MA, USA
(508) 888-0900
O

MARYLAND

Coldwell Banker
Waterman Realty Co.
109 Country Day Road, Suite 1
Chester, MD, USA
(410) 643-5005
O

Coldwell Banker
Latham, Kagan & Associates, LLC
29 Dover St.
Easton, MD, USA
(410) 822-9000
O

Coldwell Banker
Deep Creek Realty
24439 Garrett Highway
McHenry, MD, USA
(301) 387-5303
L

Coldwell Banker
Bud Church Realty, Inc.
7806 Coastal Highway
Ocean City, MD, USA
(800) 851-7326
O

Coldwell Banker
Home Realty Professionals
484 C Ritchie Highway
Severna Park, MD, USA
(410) 647-5800
O

MAINE

Coldwell Banker
American Heritage Real Estate
510 Broadway
Bangor, ME, USA
(207) 942-6773
L

Coldwell Banker
Brunette & Associates Real Estate
441 Main Street
Sanford, ME, USA
(207) 490-2900
L

Coldwell Banker
Harnden Beecher
1065 Broadway
South Portland, ME, USA
(207) 799-1501
O

Coldwell Banker
Simpson Associates, Realtors
47 Ossipee Trail East
Standish, ME, USA
(207) 642-4223
L

Market Type Designations: **M**=Mountain; **D**=Desert;
L=Lake & Stream; **O**=Ocean & Shoreline

Coldwell Banker
Thomas Agency
19 Main Street
Winthrop, ME, USA
(207) 377-2121
L

Coldwell Banker
Yorke Realty
529 U.S. Route 1, Ste #101
York, ME, USA
(207) 363-4300
O

MICHIGAN

Coldwell Banker
Schmidt, Realtors
5955 U.S. 31 North P.O. Box 15
Acme, MI, USA
(616) 938-2660
L

Coldwell Banker
Pete Stanley & Associates
314 E. Huron Road (US 23)
Au Gres, MI, USA
(517) 876-8171
LO

Coldwell Banker
North West Realty
P.O.Box 843 South M - 37
Baldwin, MI, USA
(616) 745-4646
LO

Coldwell Banker
All Seasons Realty
515 E. Cayuga St.
Bellaire, MI, USA
(616) 533-6114
LO

Coldwell Banker
All Seasons Realty
515 E Cayuga Street
Bellaire, MI, USA
(616) 533-6114
L

Coldwell Banker
Blakely Realty Co.
1630 N. State St. P.O. Box 130
Big Rapids, MI, USA
(616) 796-5823
L

Coldwell Banker
The Jackson Group
141 N. Main St. P.O. Box 656
Brooklyn, MI, USA
(517) 592-6029
L

Coldwell Banker
Schmidt, Realtors
130 Cadillac West Mall-Hwy M55
Cadillac, MI, USA
(616) 775-1737
L

Coldwell Banker
All Seasons Realty
7953 E State
Central Lake, MI, USA
(616) 544-5015
L

Coldwell Banker
Schmidt, Realtors
710 Bridge Street
Charlevoix, MI, USA
(616) 547-4444
L

Coldwell Banker
Northern Lakes
10667 N. Straits Hwy
Cheboygan, MI, USA
(616) 627-9959
LO

Coldwell Banker
Deans' P.C.
62 West Chicago St.
Coldwater, MI, USA
(517) 278-7600
L

Market Type Designations: **M**=Mountain; **D**=Desert;
L=Lake & Stream; **O**=Ocean & Shoreline

Coldwell Banker
Town & Country
4891 Wil-O-Paw Drive
Coloma, MI, USA
(616) 468-7986
L

Coldwell Banker
Pro Realty
110 North 13th Street
Escanaba, MI, USA
(906) 786-5972
LO

Coldwell Banker
Vandenberg Real Estate
1331 W. Main Street
Fremont, MI, USA
(616) 924-3050
LO

Coldwell Banker
Schmidt, Realtors
700 West Main Street
Gaylord, MI, USA
(517) 732-6777
L

Coldwell Banker
Schmidt, Realtors
6572 Western Avenue-POBox 317
Glen Arbor, MI, USA
(616) 334-3006
L

Coldwell Banker
Rycenga Real Estate
1705 S. Beacon Blvd.
Grand Haven, MI, USA
(616) 842-7550
LO

Coldwell Banker
Schmidt, Realtors
3744 28th Street SE
Grand Rapids, MI, USA
(616) 940-8000
L

Coldwell Banker
Schmidt, Realtors
3870 PLAINFIELD NE
Grand Rapids, MI, USA
(616) 365-0800
L

Coldwell Banker
Dunbar Bell & Associates
3112 N M-65
Hale, MI, USA
(517) 728-2100
LO

Coldwell Banker
Schmidt, Realtors
266 East Main Street
Harbor Springs, MI, USA
(616) 526-1100
L

Coldwell Banker
Anchor Real Estate, Inc.
218 Washington
Hart, MI, USA
(616) 873-3400
LO

Coldwell Banker
Classic Realty
319 N. Broadway
Hastings, MI, USA
(616) 945-2488
L

Coldwell Banker
Lake Forest Realty, Inc.
515 East 16th Street
Holland, MI, USA
(616) 392-5993
LO

Coldwell Banker
Jackpine Real Estate
1077 West Branch Rd Po Box 807
Houghton Lake, MI, USA
(517) 366-8848
LO

Coldwell Banker
Northern Lakes
3970 Sturgeon
Indian River, MI, USA
(616) 238-9336
LO

Coldwell Banker
The Jackson Group, Inc.
180 W Michigan Ave. 10th
Jackson, MI, USA
(517) 787-8300
L

Coldwell Banker
Lakewood
1430 Jordan Lake Street
Lake Odessa, MI, USA
(616) 374-8855
L

Coldwell Banker
Schmidt, Realtors
208 N. Main Street
Leland, MI, USA
(616) 256-9836
L

Coldwell Banker
Joachim Realty, Inc.
5517 S. Main St.
Lexington, MI, USA
(810) 359-2010
LO

Coldwell Banker
Klemm Real Estate, Inc.
905 E Ludington Ave
Ludington, MI, USA
(616) 843-3468
LO

Coldwell Banker
Northern Lakes
115 N. Huron, Box 863
Mackinaw City, MI, USA
(616)436-4151
L

Coldwell Banker
ALM Realty & Associates, Inc.
1121 Parkdale Avenue
Manistee, MI, USA
(616) 723-3555
LO

Coldwell Banker
Country House
3611 Henry Street
Muskegon, MI, USA
(616) 780-4444
LO

Coldwell Banker
Anchor Real Estate Specialists
1400 Chicago Rd.
Niles, MI, USA
(616) 683-4507
LO

Coldwell Banker
Sunrise
314 North State Street
Oscoda, MI, USA
(800) 968-1433
LO

Coldwell Banker
Shooltz Realty
932 South Lapeer Road
Oxford, MI, USA
(248) 628-4711
L

Coldwell Banker
Schmidt, Realtors
318 E. Mitchell Street
Petoskey, MI, USA
(616) 347-7600
L

Coldwell Banker
Frendt Realty, Inc.
2887 Krafft Road
Port Huron, MI, USA
(810) 987-1424
O

Market Type Designations: M=Mountain; D=Desert;
L=Lake & Stream; O=Ocean & Shoreline

Coldwell Banker
Frohm & Assoc., Realtors
8992 East D Ave.
Richland, MI, USA
(616) 629-9772
L

Coldwell Banker
Star Real Estate, Inc.
639 W. Higgins Lake Dr.
Roscommon, MI, USA
(517) 821-8585
LO

Coldwell Banker
Weber Seiler Realtors
P. O. Box 888, 455 Broadway
South Haven, MI, USA
(616) 637-1141
LO

Coldwell Banker
Joachim Realty, Inc.
515 Clinton Avenue
St. Clair, MI, USA
(810) 329-9036
LO

Coldwell Banker
Dunbar Bell & Associates
1727 North St. Helen Rd.
St. Helen, MI, USA
(517) 389-3312
LO

Coldwell Banker
Anchor Real Estate
2409 Lake Shore Drive
St. Joseph, MI, USA
(616) 983-0011
LO

Coldwell Banker
Lakes Realty
8520 100th Avenue
Stanwood, MI, USA
(616) 972-8300
L

Coldwell Banker
Abacus Real Estate
501 S Centerville Rd-POB 7008
Sturgis, MI, USA
(616) 651-4741
L

Coldwell Banker
Schmidt, Realtors
310 St. Joseph St.
Sutton`s Bay, MI, USA
(616) 271-6161
L

Coldwell Banker
Schmidt, Realtors
402 East Front Street
Traverse City, MI, USA
(616) 922-2350
LO

Coldwell Banker
Schmidt, Realtors
548 East Front Street
Traverse City, MI, USA
(616) 947-3870
L

Coldwell Banker
Dunbar Bell & Associates
2814 Cook Road, W
West Branch, MI, USA
(517) 345-3730
LO

Coldwell Banker
Dunbar Bell & Associates
3008 Rifle River Trail
West Branch, MI, USA
(517) 873-4588
L

MINNESOTA

Coldwell Banker
Crown, Realtors
625 Broadway
Alexandria, MN, USA
(320) 762-2172
L

Coldwell Banker
Elite
1204 Paul Bunyan Drive N.W.
Bemidji, MN, USA
(218) 751-1231
L

Coldwell Banker
North Country Realty
17 W. Main St.
Crosby, MN, USA
(800) 450-7150
L

Coldwell Banker
Pro IV Realty
944 S. Lake Street
Forest Lake, MN, USA
(612) 464-4101
L

Coldwell Banker
Northwoods Realty
812 Pokegama Ave
Grand Rapids, MN, USA
(218) 326-3455
L

Coldwell Banker
Choice Realty
503 Fourth Street
International Falls, MN, USA
(218) 285-7199
L

Coldwell Banker
Country Living Realty
133 S. Union
Mora, MN, USA
(320) 679-5661
L

Coldwell Banker
Backstrom & Associates
26 N. Broadway - P.O. Box C
Pelican Rapids, MN, USA
(218) 863-8723
L

Coldwell Banker
Pro IV Realty
885 7th Street
Pine City, MN, USA
(612) 222-0024
L

Coldwell Banker
Properties North
912 8th Street So. PO Box 72
Virginia, MN, USA
(218) 749-8222
L

Coldwell Banker
1st Minnesota
5th & Michigan
Walker, MN, USA
(218) 547-3600
L

Coldwell Banker
The Realty Company
1234 Oxford P.O. Box 277
Worthington, MN, USA
(507) 372-2988

MISSOURI

Coldwell Banker
Town & Country Realty, Inc.
531 Benham
Bonne Terre, MO, USA
(573) 358-3020
L

Coldwell Banker
A Blue Ribbon Realty
544 N. Business 65
Branson, MO, USA
(417) 334-1346
L

Coldwell Banker
Heritage-Kupfer
508 East Highway 54
Camdenton, MO, USA
(800) 769-2081
LO

Market Type Designations: M=Mountain; D=Desert;
L=Lake & Stream; O=Ocean & Shoreline

Coldwell Banker
Townsend Real Estate
100 Wesmor
Clinton, MO, USA
(660) 885-5959
L

Coldwell Banker
Shannon & Associates
1301 South Hwy 32
El Dorado Springs, MO, USA
(417) 876-2900
L

Coldwell Banker
First Choice, Realtors
16205 U.S. Highway 160, PO 487
Forsyth, MO, USA
(417) 546-4766
L

Coldwell Banker
 Lake St. Louis
#50 Centre on the Lake
Lake St. Louis, MO, USA
(314) 561-1000
L

Coldwell Banker
Parade of Homes
Highway 5   P.O. Box 1308
Laurie, MO, USA
(573) 374-4520
LO

Coldwell Banker
Satisfaction, Inc.
Highway 5 and F, P.O. Box 507
Sunrise Beach, MO, USA
(573) 374-7213
L

MISSISSIPPI

Coldwell Banker
Alfonso Realty, Inc.
2619 Pass Road
Biloxi, MS, USA
(601) 388-3800
O

Coldwell Banker
Coast Delta Realty
5400 Indian Hill Boulevard
Diamondhead, MS, USA
(228) 255-9188
LO

Coldwell Banker
Smith Homes, Inc., Realtors
PO Box 819, 2000 Highway 90
Gautier, MS, USA
(601) 497-1800
LO

Coldwell Banker
Lanier Sykes Bogen Realty, Inc.
157 West Reed Road
Greenville, MS, USA
(601) 334-1450
L

Coldwell Banker
Alfonso Realty, Inc.
233 Courthouse Rd
Gulfport, MS, USA
(228) 897-9000
O

Coldwell Banker
Brown/Davis, Realtors, Inc.
243 John R. Junkin Drive
Natchez, MS, USA
(601) 442-9999
LO

Coldwell Banker
Johnson Realty
6913 Washington Avenue
Ocean Springs, MS, USA
(601) 872-3330
LO

Coldwell Banker
Alfonso Realty, Inc.
117 E. Scenic Dr
Pass Christian, MS, USA
(228)452-7444
O

Market Type Designations: **M**=Mountain; **D**=Desert;
L=Lake & Stream; O=Ocean & Shoreline

MONTANA

Coldwell Banker
Wachholz & Company Real Estate
710 Grand Drive
Bigfork, MT, USA
(406) 837-1234
MLO

Coldwell Banker
The Brokers
1215 24th Street West
Billings, MT, USA
(406) 652-6100
M

Coldwell Banker
RCI Realty
2621 W. College
Bozeman, MT, USA
(406) 587-7653
M

Coldwell Banker
Wachholz & Company Real Estate
Box 2771, 1123 Highway 2
Columbia Falls, MT, USA
(406) 892-5200
MLO

Coldwell Banker
Cogswell Real Estate
800 9th St. South
Great Falls, MT, USA
(406) 727-6000
ML

Coldwell Banker
Western States Associates
115 West Main Street
Hamilton, MT, USA
(406) 363-1250
M

Coldwell Banker
Thompson-Nistler & Associates
1828 N. Main
Helena, MT, USA
(406) 443-1300
MLO

Coldwell Banker
Wachholz & Company Real Estate
P.O.Box 1475, 1205 S. Main St.
Kalispell, MT, USA
(406) 751-4300
MLO

Coldwell Banker
Maverick Realty
125 E. Callender
Livingston, MT, USA
(406) 222-0304
M

Coldwell Banker
Wachholz & Company Real Estate
105 Baker Avenue
Whitefish, MT, USA
(406) 862-4200
MLO

NORTH CAROLINA

Coldwell Banker
Spectrum Properties
515 Morehead Ave.
Atlantic Beach, NC, USA
(919) 247-5848
O

Coldwell Banker
Mountain Top Realty
Hwy184,Sugarview Bldg Unit 1&2
Banner Elk, NC, USA
(704) 898-6550
M

Coldwell Banker
The Bath Realty Network
120 S. Main Street
Bath, NC, USA
(800) 700-8910
O

Coldwell Banker
Blair & Associates
2408 Highway 105
Boone, NC, USA
(704) 262-1836
M

Market Type Designations: **M**=Mountain; **D**=Desert;
L=Lake & Stream; **O**=Ocean & Shoreline

Coldwell Banker
Melton Co., Realtors
226 S. Caldwell Street
Brevard, NC, USA
(800) 648-3309
M

Coldwell Banker
United Realty Group
1001 N. Lake Park Blvd
Carolina Beach, NC, USA
(910) 458-4401
O

Coldwell Banker
By-The-Lake Realty
1818 Hwy 16 North
Denver, NC, USA
(704) 483-1518
L

Coldwell Banker
Spectrum Properties
7413 Emerald Drive
Emerald Isle, NC, USA
(919) 354-3070
O

Coldwell Banker
United Realty
3800 Raeford Road
Fayetteville, NC, USA
(910) 483-5353
L

Coldwell Banker
Daniel Seay and Associates
426 Porter Street
Franklin, NC, USA
(704) 369-7369
M

Coldwell Banker
First Realty
102 Roosevelt Blvd.
Havelock, NC, USA
(919) 444-3333
O

Coldwell Banker
Nichols, Jones & Associates, Inc.
622 NC 69
Hayesville, NC, USA
(800) 767-1608
M

Coldwell Banker
Wester Realty
1020 South Garnett Street
Henderson, NC, USA
(919) 438-8099
L

Coldwell Banker
Ashburn Real Estate
P.O. Box 2805
Highlands, NC, USA
(704) 526-4151
M

Coldwell Banker
Ockuly Realty Company
99 Marine Blvd S.
Jacksonville, NC, USA
(910) 455-2977
O

Coldwell Banker
Conway & Company, Realtors
707 Plaza Boulevard
Kinston, NC, USA
(919) 522-1911
L

Coldwell Banker
Fairfield Mountain Realty
2014 Buffalo Creek Road
Lake Lure, NC, USA
(704) 625-2020
M

Coldwell Banker
Lake Norman Associates
307 Williamson Rd
Mooresville, NC, USA
(704) 664-5253
L

Market Type Designations: M=Mountain; D=Desert;
L=Lake & Stream; O=Ocean & Shoreline

Coldwell Banker
Newton Real Estate Inc.
214 Avery Avenue
Morganton, NC, USA
(704) 433-1485
M

Coldwell Banker
Coastline Realty
965 Old Folkstone Rd. Ste. 108
Sneads Ferry, NC, USA
(910) -327-7711
O

Coldwell Banker
Willis-Smith Company
115 Middle Street
New Bern, NC, USA
(919) 638-3500
O

Coldwell Banker
Prime Resort Real Estate
110 Commerce Avenue
Southern Pines, NC, USA
(800) 692-8088
L

Coldwell Banker
Southport-Oak Island Realty
300 Country Club Drive
Oak Island, NC, USA
(910) 278-3311
O

Coldwell Banker
Southport-Oak Island Realty
607 North Howe Street
Southport, NC, USA
(910) 457-6713
O

Coldwell Banker
Harbour Realty
901 Broad Street
Oriental, NC, USA
(800) 326-3748
O

Coldwell Banker
Town & Country, Realtors
937 South Trade Street
Tryon, NC, USA
(704) 859-5806
M

Coldwell Banker
Groce Real Estate
1508 So Horner Blvd
Sanford, NC, USA
(919) 775-5548
L

Coldwell Banker
Baker Properties
6336 Oleander Drive, Ste 1
Wilmington, NC, USA
(910) 395-5566
O

Coldwell Banker
Groce Real Estate
3713 Highway 87 South
Sanford, NC, USA
(919) 498-1230
L

Coldwell Banker
Baker Properties
25 Market Street
Wilmington, NC, USA
(910) 251-2234
O

Coldwell Banker
Horn And Associates, Inc.
213 S. Dekalb Street
Shelby, NC, USA
(704) 482-7316
L

Coldwell Banker
Hanover Realty, Inc.
3901 Oleander Drive E & F
Wilmington, NC, USA
(910) 395-2244
O

Market Type Designations: M=Mountain; D=Desert;
L=Lake & Stream; O=Ocean & Shoreline

Coldwell Banker
Sea Coast Realty
5710 Oleander Drive, Suite 200
Wilmington, NC, USA
(800) 522-9624
O

NEBRASKA

Coldwell Banker
Town & Country Realty of
Hastings, Inc.
700 E. Side Blvd.
Hastings, NE, USA
(402) 463-4591
L

Coldwell Banker
Dover Realtors
1000 Norfolk Avenue
Norfolk, NE, USA
(402) 371-0200
O

NEW HAMPSHIRE

Coldwell Banker
Steve Weeks, Realtors
348 Court Street
Laconia, NH, USA
(603) 524-2255
ML

Coldwell Banker
Golden & Covey, Realtors
222 Main Street
Littleton, NH, USA
(603) 444-6737
M

Coldwell Banker
Milestone Real Estate
P.O Box 67, 177 Main St.
New London, NH, USA
(603) 526-4116
ML

Coldwell Banker
Old Mill Properties
One Holderness Road
Plymouth, NH, USA
(603) 536-3333
ML

Coldwell Banker
Hunneman & Company
254 State Street
Portsmouth, NH, USA
(617) 426-4260
O

Coldwell Banker
Hobin Realty
1257 Washington Rd At Rt1
Rye, NH, USA
(603) 964-1800
O

NEW JERSEY

Coldwell Banker
Basking Ridge/Harding
374 N. Maple Ave
Basking Ridge, NJ, USA
(908) 766-4433
L

Coldwell Banker
Riviera Realty, Inc.
550 Brick Boulevard
Brick, NJ, USA
(732) 477-2000
O

Coldwell Banker
Sol Needles Real Estate
512 Washington Mall
Cape May, NJ, USA
(609) 884-8428
O

Coldwell Banker
Fair Haven
636 River Road
Fair Haven, NJ, USA
(732) 842-7600
O

Coldwell Banker
Red Top Realty
824 Radio Road
Little Egg Harbor, NJ, USA
(609) 296-3602
O

Coldwell Banker
Sand Dollar Real Estate
1601 North Bay Avenue
North Beach Haven, NJ, USA
(609) 492-0990
O

Coldwell Banker
Laricks Real Estate
4110 Landis Avenue
Sea Isle City, NJ, USA
(609) 263-8300
O

Coldwell Banker
Sparta
1 Professional Quadrangle
Sparta, NJ, USA
(973)729-6131
ML

Coldwell Banker
Faline, Inc., Realtors
Route 515; P.O. Box 458
Vernon, NJ, USA
(201) 764-6121
M

Coldwell Banker
Vernon
546 Route 515
Vernon, NJ, USA
(973) 764-4085
ML

Coldwell Banker
Wall Township
2051 Highway 35
Wall Township, NJ, USA
(732) 449-0093
O

NEW MEXICO

Coldwell Banker
Parnegg Metro
6767 Academy Road N.E.
Albuquerque, NM, USA
(505) 828-1000
D

Coldwell Banker
Parnegg Metro
12042 N. Highway 14
Cedar Crest, NM, USA
(505) 281-0000
M

Coldwell Banker
SDC, Realtors
307 Mechem Dr.
Ruidoso, NM, USA
(505) 257-5111
M

Coldwell Banker
Trails West Realty, Ltd.
2000 Old Pecos Trail
Santa Fe, NM, USA
(505) 988-7285
M

Coldwell Banker
Lota Realty, Inc.
102 N. Pueblo Road
Taos, NM, USA
(505) 758-8673
M

NEVADA

Coldwell Banker
Anchor Realty, Inc.
Box 60367, 1497 Nevada Hwy., S
Boulder City, NV, USA
(702) 293-5757
D

Coldwell Banker
Nannini Realty
820 Idaho Street
Elko, NV, USA
(702) 738-4078
D

174   Market Type Designations: M=Mountain; D=Desert;
L=Lake & Stream; O=Ocean & Shoreline

Coldwell Banker
West & Associates
85 E. Main St.
Fernley, NV, USA
(702) 575-5522
MDL

Coldwell Banker
Incline Village Realty, Inc.
Box 3549, 795 Mays Blvd.
Incline Village, NV, USA
(702) 831-1515
ML

Coldwell Banker
Bowser Realty & Associates
Box 10829, 613 Highway #50
Zephyr Cove, NV, USA
(702) 588-6241
ML

NEW YORK

Coldwell Banker
First Properties
8395 Oswego Road
Baldwinsville, NY, USA
(315) 652-3522
L

Coldwell Banker
Bedford
30 Village Green
Bedford, NY, USA
(914) 234-3647
L

Coldwell Banker
King George Realty
Lake Shore Drive; P.O. Box 777
Bolton Landing, NY, USA
(518) 644-2243
LO

Coldwell Banker
Gabriel Premier Properties
220 Groton Avenue
Cortland, NY, USA
(607) 756-9854
M

Coldwell Banker
All-Bridge Realty
245 E. Main Street
Elbridge, NY, USA
(315) 689-3926
L

Coldwell Banker
Square 1 Real Estate
192 East Main St
Fredonia, NY, USA
(716) 672-7990
MLO

Coldwell Banker
Genesee Valley Properties
4400 Lakeville Road
Geneseo, NY, USA
(716) 243-9140
L

Coldwell Banker
Parrott-Venuti Real Estate, Inc.
218 Hamilton Street
Geneva, NY, USA
(315) 789-6768
L

Coldwell Banker
Dunes View Properties
20 West Montauk Hwy
Hampton Bays, NY, USA
(516) 728-2300
O

Coldwell Banker
Helling Real Estate
12 West Main Street, PO Box 72
Honeoye, NY, USA
(716) 229-5000
L

Coldwell Banker
Shaw Real Estate
413 North Tioga St
Ithaca, NY, USA
(607) 272-4777
ML

Market Type Designations: M=Mountain; D=Desert;
L=Lake & Stream; O=Ocean & Shoreline

Coldwell Banker
Phil Mathyer Real Estate
828 Fairmount Ave WE
Jamestown, NY, USA
(716) 483-0065
ML

Coldwell Banker
Arlene M. Sitterly, Inc.
363 North Comrie Avenue
Johnstown, NY, USA
(518) 762-9885
ML

Coldwell Banker
 Larchmont
140 Larchmont Avenue
Larchmont, NY, USA
(914) 834-3505
O

Coldwell Banker
Beach West Realty
880 West Beech Street
Long Beach, NY, USA
(516) 889-7500
O

Coldwell Banker
First Properties
216 Fayette Street
Manlius, NY, USA
(315) 682-7197
L

Coldwell Banker
Timberland Properties
Box 667 Bridge Street
Margaretville, NY, USA
(914) 586-3321
M

Coldwell Banker
Celic
Main Road Celic Center, P.O. B
Mattituck, NY, USA
(516) 298-8000
O

Coldwell Banker
Currier & Lazier, Realtors
280 Route 211 East
Middletown, NY, USA
(914) 342-5766
M

Coldwell Banker
Timm Associates
P.O. Box 101 Main Street
Old Forge, NY, USA
(315) 369-3951
ML

Coldwell Banker
Midlakes Properties
230 B Lake Street Plaza
Penn Yan, NY, USA
(315) 536-6369
ML

Coldwell Banker
First American Real Estate
1170 Pittsford-Victor Rd.
Pittsford, NY, USA
(716) 248-5800
L

Coldwell Banker
Community Group
468 Empire Boulevard
Rochester, NY, USA
(716) 482-4800
LO

Coldwell Banker
Royal Oak Realty
1429 Ridge Road West
Rochester, NY, USA
(716) 865-6000
L

Coldwell Banker
Select Properties
1685 Monroe Avenue
Rochester, NY, USA
(716) 442-8090
L

Market Type Designations: M=Mountain; D=Desert;
L=Lake & Stream; O=Ocean & Shoreline

Coldwell Banker
1st Rome Realty
1006 Black River Blvd
Rome, NY, USA
(315) 337-4390
M

Coldwell Banker
First Properties
5854 Belle Isle Road
Syracuse, NY, USA
(315) 488-2926
L

Coldwell Banker
Dendis Real Estate
15 West Main Street
Waterloo, NY, USA
(315) 539-9282
L

Coldwell Banker
Rimada Realty
1063-C Arsenal Street
Watertown, NY, USA
(315) 788-4444
MLO

Coldwell Banker
Dunes View Properties
148 Main Street
Westhampton Beach, NY, USA
(516) 288-0400
O

Coldwell Banker
Pultney Land Company
4062 West Main Street
Williamson, NY, USA
(315) 589-9676
LO

OHIO

Coldwell Banker
Ward Real Estate, Inc.
600 E. Main
Ashland, OH, USA
(419) 281-2000
L

Coldwell Banker
Lake Shore
222 East Market Street
Celina, OH, USA
(419) 586-6427
LO

Coldwell Banker
Top Lake
7409 SR 366 Indian Lake
Huntsville, OH, USA
(937) 842-6666
LO

Coldwell Banker
Megatrend Realty, Inc.
850 E. Main St.
Lancaster, OH, USA
(740) 687-5223
L

Coldwell Banker
Mullendore, Realtors
100 South Gay Street
Mount Vernon, OH, USA
(614) 397-8800
L

Coldwell Banker
New Towne Realty, Ltd.
255 Second Street N.E.
New Philadelphia, OH, USA
(330) 343-7600
L

Coldwell Banker
Routh Realty
3313 Milan Road
Sandusky, OH, USA
(800) 626-9995
LO

OKLAHOMA

Coldwell Banker
Ted Goforth & Associates
Box 755, HC63 Box 13
Eufaula, OK, USA
(918) 689-9797
L

Market Type Designations: **M**=Mountain; **D**=Desert;
L=Lake & Stream; **O**=Ocean & Shoreline

Coldwell Banker
Santa Fe Realty
100 North 5th Street
McAlester, OK, USA
(918) 423-6888
L

OREGON

Coldwell Banker
Oregon Coast Realty
Box 610, 703 Chetco Ave.
Brookings, OR, USA
(800) 342-9405
LO

Coldwell Banker
Kent Price Realty, Inc.
139 West 2nd Street
Cannon Beach, OR, USA
(503) 436-1171
LO

Coldwell Banker
Justrom & Stromme, Inc., Realtors
543 S. 4th Street
Coos Bay, OR, USA
(541) 267-7078
LO

Coldwell Banker
Ritter & Associates
115 Tejaka Lane
Enterprise, OR, USA
(541) 426-3104
ML

Coldwell Banker
1st Florence Real Estate
Box 2227, 398 Hwy. 101
Florence, OR, USA
(541) 997-8288
LO

Coldwell Banker
Gesik Realty, Inc.
6645 Gleneden Beach Loop Rd.
Gleneden Beach, OR, USA
(541) 764-5030
LO

Coldwell Banker
Whitehead Real Estate
29441 Ellensburg
Gold Beach, OR, USA
(541) 247-4518
LO

Coldwell Banker
Doran Taylor, Inc.
550 Northeast E St.
Grants Pass, OR, USA
(541) 479-8331
M

Coldwell Banker
Holman Realty, Inc.
4729 South 6th St.
Klamath Falls, OR, USA
(541) 884-1343
ML

Coldwell Banker
Valley Brokers
2600 S. Santiam Hwy.
Lebanon, OR, USA
(541) 451-4513
L

Coldwell Banker
Gesik Realty, Inc.
1815 NW Highway 101
Lincoln City, OR, USA
(541) 994-7760
LO

Coldwell Banker
Kent Price Realty, Inc.
Box 338, 31 Laneda
Manzanita, OR, USA
(800) 256-1719
LO

Coldwell Banker
1st Newport Realty
306 East Olive St
Newport, OR, USA
(541) 265-2345
LO

Market Type Designations: **M**=Mountain; **D**=Desert;
L=Lake & Stream; **O**=Ocean & Shoreline

Coldwell Banker
Kent Price Realty, Inc.
2367 S. Holladay Drive
Seaside, OR, USA
(800) 829-0419
LO

Coldwell Banker
Reed Bros. Realty
Box 219, 291 W. Cascade Ave.
Sisters, OR, USA
(541) 549-6000
ML

Coldwell Banker
First Resort Realty
Sunriver Village Bldg. 9
Sunriver, OR, USA
(541) 593-1234
L

Coldwell Banker
Evergreen Realty
1180 Highway 101 North
Tillamook, OR, USA
(503) 842-0101
LO

Coldwell Banker
Miller's Real Estate Services, Inc.
Box 787, 585 Hemlock
Waldport, OR, USA
(541) 563-2349
LO

Coldwell Banker
Miller's Real Estate Services, Inc.
665 HWY 101 North
Yachats, OR, USA
(541) 547-3171
LO

PENNSYLVANIA

Coldwell Banker
Town & Country Real Estate
300 Union Avenue
Altoona, PA, USA
(814) 946-4343
L

Coldwell Banker
SKS Realty
RD #5 Box 337
Bedford, PA, USA
(814) 623-7009
M

Coldwell Banker
Developac Realty
998 Beaver Drive
DuBois, PA, USA
(814) 375-1167
L

Coldwell Banker
Froehlich, Realtors
2961 Peach Street
Erie, PA, USA
(814) 453-4578
L

Coldwell Banker
Froehlich, Realtors
4664 West 12th Street
Erie, PA, USA
(814) 838-2299
L

Coldwell Banker
Country Heritage Real Estate
RD #1, Box 33D
Huntingdon, PA, USA
(814) 627-1912
L

Coldwell Banker
Bainbridge Kaufman
Real Estate, Inc.
1103 Park Avenue
Meadville, PA, USA
(814) 724-1100
M

Coldwell Banker
Rita Halverson, Realtor
555 East Main Street
Somerset, PA, USA
(814) 443-4858
M

Market Type Designations: M=Mountain; D=Desert;
L=Lake & Stream; O=Ocean & Shoreline

Coldwell Banker
Phyllis Rubin Real Estate
1250 N. Ninth Street
Stroudsburg, PA, USA
(717) 424-6611
M

Coldwell Banker
J. Ferrario Real Estate
RR#6 Box 6170
Towanda, PA, USA
(717) 265-4142
M

Coldwell Banker
Laurel Ridge Realty
554 Morgantown Street
Uniontown, PA, USA
(724) 437-7100
M

RHODE ISLAND

Coldwell Banker
Gold, Realtors
541 Hope Street
Bristol, RI, USA
(800) 543-7531
O

Coldwell Banker
Gold, Realtors
808 Tiogue Avenue
Coventry, RI, USA
(401) 437-2112
O

Coldwell Banker
Gold, Realtors
1022 Reservoir Avenue
Cranston, RI, USA
(800) 543-7531
O

Coldwell Banker
Gold, Realtors
2343 Diamond Hill Road
Cumberland, RI, USA
(800) 543-7531
O

Coldwell Banker
Gold, Realtors
694 Main Street
East Greenwich, RI, USA
(800) 543-7531
O

Coldwell Banker
Gold, Realtors
7291 Post Road
North Kingstown, RI, USA
(800) 543-7531
O

Coldwell Banker
Gold, Realtors
55 South Angell Street
Providence - East Side, RI, USA
(401) 437-2112
O

Coldwell Banker
Gold, Realtors
1445 Wampanoag Trail
Riverside, RI, USA
(401) 437-1800
O

Coldwell Banker
Gold, Realtors
265 Putnam Pike
Smithfield, RI, USA
(800) 543-7531
O

Coldwell Banker
Gold, Realtors
2181 Post Road
Warwick, RI, USA
(401) 437-2112
O

Coldwell Banker
Cahoone, Realtors
29 Post Rd
Westerly, RI, USA
(401) 596-6333
O

Market Type Designations: **M**=Mountain; **D**=Desert;
L=Lake & Stream; **O**=Ocean & Shoreline

SOUTH CAROLINA

Coldwell Banker
Preferred Realty
3098 Whiskey Road
Aiken, SC, USA
(803) 649-5333
L

Coldwell Banker
Durham-Meehan Company, Inc.
1008 N. Main Street
Anderson, SC, USA
(864) 225-3788
L

Coldwell Banker
Carteret Properties, Inc.
705 Carteret Street
Beaufort, SC, USA
(803) 521-4500
O

Coldwell Banker
Tom Jenkins Realty, Inc.
119 Amick's Ferry Road
Chapin, SC, USA
(803) 799-HOME
L

Coldwell Banker
Tom Jenkins Realty, Inc.
1136 Washington Street, #700
Columbia, SC, USA
(803) 799-HOME
L

Coldwell Banker
Associated Agents, Inc.
119 Waccamaw Med Park Dr
Conway, SC, USA
(803) 347-3181
O

Coldwell Banker
The Lesley Agency
712 South Pendleton Street
Easley, SC, USA
(864) 859-5150
M

Coldwell Banker
Sea Island Realty
547 Hwy 174, P. O. Box 40
Edisto Island, SC, USA
(803) 869-3163
O

Coldwell Banker
Toon Pawley Real Estate, Inc.
71F Pope Ave.
Hilton Head Island, SC, USA
(800) 845-3520
O

Coldwell Banker
Tom Jenkins Realty, Inc.
5551 Sunset Blvd.
Lexington, SC, USA
(803) 799-HOME
L

Coldwell Banker
Associated Agents, Inc.
315 Highway 17, North Surfside
Myrtle Beach, SC, USA
(803) 238-3181
O

Coldwell Banker
Preferred Properties
3901 N. Kings Highway
Myrtle Beach, SC, USA
(803) 444-0777
O

Coldwell Banker
Leonard, Roberts Real Estate.
14792 Ocean Highway, North Lit
Pawley's Island, SC, USA
(843) 237-1686
O

Coldwell Banker
Pat Williams Realty
230 Plaza Circle PO Box 525
Santee, SC, USA
(803) 854-2119
L

Market Type Designations: M=Mountain; D=Desert;
L=Lake & Stream; O=Ocean & Shoreline

Coldwell Banker
Durham-Meehan Company, Inc.
450B 123 Bypass Keowee Center
Seneca, SC, USA
(864) 882-0168
L

Coldwell Banker
Ulmer-Carolina
P.O. Box 1702
Walterboro, SC, USA
(803) 549-6928
O

SOUTH DAKOTA

Coldwell Banker
Folkerts Realty
407 North Main
Mitchell, SD, USA
(605) 996-7747
L

Coldwell Banker
Lewis-Kirkeby-Hall Real Estate Inc.
2700 West Main
Rapid City, SD, USA
(605) 343-2700
M

Coldwell Banker
GKR & Associates
1000 East 41st Street
Sioux Falls, SD, USA
(605) 339-9100
LO

Coldwell Banker
Roby Agency, Realtors
818 S. Broadway, P.O. Box 1025
Watertown, SD, USA
(605) 886-0000
L

Coldwell Banker
Anderson Realty, L.L.C.
122 West Third
Yankton, SD, USA
(605) 665-7407
LO

TENNESSEE

Coldwell Banker
GSM Realty
490 East Parkway
Gatlinburg, TN, USA
(800) 445-6705
M

Coldwell Banker
Lakeside, Realtors
530 West Main Street
Hendersonville, TN, USA
(615) 824-5920
L

Coldwell Banker
Lakeside, Realtors
3735 North Mount Juliet Road
Mount Juliet, TN, USA
(615) 758-0488
L

Coldwell Banker
GSM Realty
1000 Parkway
Sevierville, TN, USA
(423) 428-1636
M

TEXAS

Coldwell Banker
Myers-Gallagher
264 South Commercial
Aransas Pass, TX, USA
(512) 758-7534
LO

Coldwell Banker
F M I Realty
200 E. Russell
Bonham, TX, USA
(903) 583-4471
L

Coldwell Banker
Island, Realtors
14613 S. Padre Island Drive
Corpus Christi, TX, USA
(512) 949-7077
O

Market Type Designations: M=Mountain; D=Desert;
L=Lake & Stream; O=Ocean & Shoreline

Coldwell Banker
Realty Connection
124 Mall Drive
Corsicana, TX, USA
(903) 874-7171
L

Coldwell Banker
Lighthouse Realty
8610 Seawall Ste 230
Galveston, TX, USA
(409) 740-4040
O

Coldwell Banker
Real Estate Exchange
726 Elm Street
Graham, TX, USA
(940) 549-2970
L

Coldwell Banker
American Dream Realty
600 W. Main
Gun Barrel City, TX, USA
(800) 594-7993
L

Coldwell Banker
Pennington-Chen Real Estate
1120 Bay Area Blvd.
Houston, TX, USA
(281) 486-9770
L

Coldwell Banker
The Hancock Company
Box 398, 1202 W. Church
Livingston, TX, USA
(409) 327-3080
L

Coldwell Banker
On Lake Conroe
23105 Hwy 105 West
Montgomery, TX, USA
(409) 448-2100
L

Coldwell Banker
Island, Realtors
821 Alister Street
Port Aransas, TX, USA
(512) 749-6000
O

Coldwell Banker
Benchmark, Realtors
421 N. Sam Rayburn Fwy.
Sherman, TX, USA
(903) 893-8174
L

Coldwell Banker
Goodman Assoc.
3100 Padre Blvd.
South Padre Island, TX, USA
(800) 55-PADRE
O

Coldwell Banker
Kennedy & Associates
1325 So Broadway
Sulphur Springs, TX, USA
(903) 885-1563
L

Coldwell Banker
At Lake Whitney Realty
Box 2007, 100 E. Jefferson
Whitney, TX, USA
(254) 694-5374
L

UTAH

Coldwell Banker
Tugaw, Realtors
176 North Main
Brigham City, UT, USA
(800) 894-9492
M

Coldwell Banker
Gold Key Realty, Inc.
135 South Main
Logan, UT, USA
(801) 753-8824
M

Market Type Designations: M=Mountain; D=Desert;
L=Lake & Stream; O=Ocean & Shoreline

Coldwell Banker
Arches Realty
150 E. Center St.
Moab, UT, USA
(801) 259-5693
M

Coldwell Banker
Premier Realty
1750 Park Avenue
Park City, UT, USA
(435) 649-4400
M

Coldwell Banker
West Realty
455 N. University Avenue #201
Provo, UT, USA
(801) 377-8140
ML

VIRGINIA

Coldwell Banker
Owens & Co
325 Cummings Dr
Abingdon, VA, USA
(540) 628-9330
ML

Coldwell Banker
Harbour Realty
22639 Center Pkwy   PO Box 616
Accomac, VA, USA
(757) 787-1305
O

Coldwell Banker
Holdren, Eubank & Stanley
158 West Main Street
Bedford, VA, USA
(540) 586-1000
M

Coldwell Banker
Bailey Realty Co.
1455 East Rio Rd; PO Box 6700
Charlottesville, VA, USA
(804) 973-9555
M

Coldwell Banker
Lafoon Realty, Inc.
720 Oak Street
Farmville, VA, USA
(804) 392-6191
ML

Coldwell Banker
Premier Properties
907 North Royal Avenue
Front Royal, VA, USA
(540) 636-7700
M

Coldwell Banker
Horsley And Constable
66 South Court Square
Harrisonburg, VA, USA
(540) 434-7373
M

Coldwell Banker
Fred Hetzel & Associates, Inc.
17 Loudoun Street SE
Leesburg, VA, USA
(703) 777-5500
M

Coldwell Banker
Colonna & Associates
25 South Main Street
Lexington, VA, USA
(540) 463-7157
M

Coldwell Banker
Panorama Realty, Inc.
PO Box 146; 1204 E. Main St.
Luray, VA, USA
(540) 743-4545
M

Coldwell Banker
Forehand & Co., Realtors
2508 Langhorne Road
Lynchburg, VA, USA
(804) 847-7731
ML

Market Type Designations: M=Mountain; D=Desert;
L=Lake & Stream; O=Ocean & Shoreline

Coldwell Banker
Countryside, Realtors
17 Bridgewater Plaza
Moneta, VA, USA
(540) 721-3323
ML

Coldwell Banker
Panorama Realty, Inc.
9398 Congress Street
New Market, VA, USA
(540) 740-4195
M

Coldwell Banker
Gifford Realty, Inc.
1547 E Little Creek Rd
Norfolk, VA, USA
(757) 583-1000
O

Coldwell Banker
Premier, Realtors
2155 Electric Road, Suite A
Roanoke, VA, USA
(540) 774-2288
M

Coldwell Banker
Farrar Realty
514 E. Atlantic Street
South Hill, VA, USA
(804) 447-8774
O

Coldwell Banker
Helfant Realty, Inc., Realtors
3300 Virginia Beach Blvd
Virginia Beach, VA, USA
(757) 463-1212
O

Coldwell Banker
Barger Real Estate
121 South Wayne Ave, Box 700
Waynesboro, VA, USA
(540) 943-1200
M

Coldwell Banker
Premier Properties
1682 S. Pleasant Valley Road
Winchester, VA, USA
(540) 662-4500
ML

Coldwell Banker
Gregory Jarvis Real Estate
110 East Main Street
Wytheville, VA, USA
(540) 228-2030
ML

VERMONT

Coldwell Banker
Islands Realty, Inc.
POB 20 - 9 South Main Street
Alburg, VT, USA
(802) 796-3426
LO

Coldwell Banker
Hickok & Boardman Realty
PO Box 1064 346 Shelburne Rd.
Burlington, VT, USA
(802) 863-1500
L

Coldwell Banker
Realty Mart
22 Main Street
Essex Jct, VT, USA
(802) 878-5600
L

Coldwell Banker
Mountain Properties, Inc.
194 Main St
Ludlow, VT, USA
(802) 228-5678
M

Coldwell Banker
Bill Beck Real Estate
20 Seymour St.; P.O. Box 533
Middlebury, VT, USA
(802) 388-7983
L

Coldwell Banker
Spademan Associates
50 Main Street
Quechee, VT, USA
(802) 295-9500
ML

Coldwell Banker
Accent Realty
182 Woodstock Avenue
Rutland, VT, USA
(802) 773-3500
M

Coldwell Banker
Islands Realty, Inc.
P.O. Box 122 U.S. Route 2
South Hero, VT, USA
(802) 372-5777
LO

Coldwell Banker
Poquette & Bruley, Inc.
112 N. Main St.
St. Albans, VT, USA
(802) 524-9526
LO

Coldwell Banker
Bill Beck Real Estate
268 Main Street
Vergennes, VT, USA
(802) 877-3125
L

WASHINGTON

Coldwell Banker
First Harbor Real Estate, Inc.
110 West Market St, Suite 100
Aberdeen, WA, USA
(360) 532-2610
O

Coldwell Banker
Marie Gallagher & Associates
337 High School Road
Bainbridge Island, WA, USA
(206) 842-1733
O

Coldwell Banker
Miller Arnason
3610 Meridian St.
Bellingham, WA, USA
(360) 734-3420
LO

Coldwell Banker
Orcas Island
P.O. BOX 127
Eastsound, WA, USA
(360) 376-2114
O

Coldwell Banker
Hawkins-Poe, Realtors
1215 Regents Blvd.
Fircrest, WA, USA
(253) 564-5252
O

Coldwell Banker
Tara Properties
Box 760, 1504 East Highway 525
Freeland, WA, USA
(360) 331-6300
O

Coldwell Banker
San Juan Islands, Inc.
Box 100, 105 Spring St.
Friday Harbor, WA, USA
(360) 378-2101
O

Coldwell Banker
Tara Properties
Box 205, 221 Second Street
Langley, WA, USA
(360) 221-1700
O

Coldwell Banker
Lopez Island, Inc.
Box 147, One Weeks Point Rd.
Lopez, WA, USA
(800) 472-3311
O

Market Type Designations: M=Mountain; D=Desert;
L=Lake & Stream; O=Ocean & Shoreline

Coldwell Banker
Koetje Real Estate
415 SE Pioneer Way
Oak Harbor, WA, USA
(800) 869-7129
O

Coldwell Banker
Tara Properties
35 SE Ely St.
Oak Harbor, WA, USA
(360) 675-7200
O

Coldwell Banker
First Harbor Real Estate, Inc.
Box 1089, 837 Point Brown Ave.
Ocean Shores, WA, USA
(360) 289-3373
O

Coldwell Banker
Uptown Realty
330 E. First St., Suite 1
Port Angeles, WA, USA
(360) 452-7861
MO

Coldwell Banker
Forrest Aldrich, Inc.
9522 Oak Bay Road, Suite 100
Port Ludlow, WA, USA
(360) 437-2278
MO

Coldwell Banker
Park Shore Real Estate
4235 SE Mile Hill Dr.
Port Orchard, WA, USA
(360) 871-2332
MO

Coldwell Banker
Forrest Aldrich, Inc.
2313 E. Sims Way
Port Townsend, WA, USA
(360) 385-4111
MO

Coldwell Banker
Bain Associates
1200 Westlake Ave. N. #406
Seattle, WA, USA
(206) 283-5200
ML

Coldwell Banker
Uptown Realty
583 W. Washington, Suite A
Sequim, WA, USA
(360) 683-6000
O

Coldwell Banker
Pacific Property Realty
SouthEast 66 Lynch Road
Shelton,WA, USA
(360) 426-7766
O

Coldwell Banker
Bayshore Realty
Box 109, 700 W. Robert Bush Dr
South Bend, WA, USA
(800) 729-4884
O

Coldwell Banker
Davenport, Realtors
135 N. Mission
Wenatchee, WA, USA
(509) 662-4521
MDL

Coldwell Banker
Winthrop Realty
503 Highway 20--PO Box 100
Winthrop, WA, USA
(509) 996-2121
ML

Coldwell Banker
Associated, Realtors
415 N. First Street
Yakima, WA, USA
(509) 248-5050
MD

Market Type Designations: M=Mountain; D=Desert;
L=Lake & Stream; O=Ocean & Shoreline

WISCONSIN

Coldwell Banker
Belva M. Parr Realty, Inc.
700 South Main Street
Adams, WI, USA
(608) 339-6757
L

Coldwell Banker
S.U.R.E. Realty Co.
816 Superior Street
Antigo, WI, USA
(715) 627-4885
L

Coldwell Banker
The Real Estate Group, Inc.
2711 N. Mason St
Appleton, WI, USA
(920) 993-7002
L

Coldwell Banker
Mc Gann Realty
1025 Eighth Street
Baraboo, WI, USA
(608) 356-6644
L

Coldwell Banker
Uptown Realty
304 Main Street
Black River Falls, WI, USA
(715) 284-9055
L

Coldwell Banker
Mulleady Inc., Realtors
226 Pine St Hwy 70 W., Box 1029
Eagle River, WI, USA
(715) 479-1774
L

Coldwell Banker
Door County Horizons
4086 Highway 42
Fish Creek, WI, USA
(920) 868-2373
LO

Coldwell Banker
Frontier Realty
P.O. B 866, Hwy 27 at Michigan
Hayward, WI, USA
(715) 634-8977
L

Coldwell Banker
Barbour, Realtors
118 South 7th Street
La Crosse, WI, USA
(608) 784-9930
L

Coldwell Banker
Geneva Lakes Area Realtors
838 Main Street
Lake Geneva, WI, USA
(414) 248-1020
L

Coldwell Banker
X-Sell Realty
1100 South 30th St., Suite 7
Manitowoc, WI, USA
(920) 682-0018
L

Coldwell Banker
Mulleady Inc., Realtors
8262 Highway 51 S P.O. Bx 1030
Minocqua, WI, USA
(800) 472-3410
L

Coldwell Banker
Kravick Realty
120 Central Avenue PO Box 5
Montello, WI, USA
(608) 297-7734
L

Coldwell Banker
The Real Estate Group, Inc.
209 St. Johns
New London, WI, USA
(414) 982-3762
L

Market Type Designations: M=Mountain; D=Desert;
L=Lake & Stream; O=Ocean & Shoreline

Coldwell Banker
Valley Real Estate
204 S Knowles Ave.
New Richmond, WI, USA
(715) 246-4567
L

Coldwell Banker
Schwab Realty, Ltd.
2129 Jackson Street
Oshkosh, WI, USA
(800) 236-4184
LO

Coldwell Banker
Larson Realty
Highway 13 South P.O. Box 108
Park Falls, WI, USA
(715) 762-2232
L

Coldwell Banker
Home Hunters Realty
501 E. Main Street
Reedsburg, WI, USA
(608) 524-2266
L

Coldwell Banker
Mulleady Inc., Realtors
1 East Courtney P.O. Box 816
Rhinelander, WI, USA
(800) 472-7334
L

Coldwell Banker
Brenizer, Realtors
237 S. Main St.
Rice Lake, WI, USA
(715) 234-5010
L

Coldwell Banker
Hilgenberg Realtors
105 S. Washington Street
Shawano, WI, USA
(715) 526-6148
L

Coldwell Banker
Van-Vleck Clemens
11427 S. Bus Hwy 53/Box 322
Solon Springs, WI, USA
(715) 378-2668
L

Coldwell Banker
Frontier Realty
Hwy 70 P.O. Box 69
Stone Lake, WI, USA
(715) 865-6411
L

Coldwell Banker
Van-Vleck Clemens
3215 Tower Avenue
Superior, WI, USA
(715) 394-6637
L

Coldwell Banker
Lake-Land Realty
1310 N. 4th St. P.O. Box 40
Tomahawk, WI, USA
(715) 453-2082
L

Coldwell Banker
Lake & Country, Realtors
336 Main Street
Twin Lakes, WI, USA
(414) 877-2131
L

Coldwell Banker
The Real Estate Group, Inc.
122 S. Main Street
Waupaca, WI, USA
(715) 258-3221
L

Coldwell Banker
Freund
309 East Main Street
Waupun, WI, USA
(920) 324-5015
LO

Market Type Designations: M=Mountain; D=Desert;
L=Lake & Stream; O=Ocean & Shoreline

Coldwell Banker
Classic
118 N. Saint Marie Street
Wautoma, WI, USA
(920) 787-1626
L

Coldwell Banker
Lakeside Realty
25941 Highway 35 South
Webster, WI, USA
(715) 866-4246
L

Coldwell Banker
Kravick Realty
109 S. Main Street PO Box 185
Westfield, WI, USA
(608) 296-2462
L

Coldwell Banker
Siewert Realtors
325 Eighth Street South
Wisconsin Rapids, WI, USA
(715) 424-4800
L

Coldwell Banker
Mulleady Inc., Realtors
1004 First Ave
Woodruff, WI, USA
(715) 356-9897
L

WEST VIRGINIA

Coldwell Banker
Raleigh Real Estate Center
600 South Oakwood Avenue
Beckley, WV, USA
(304) 255-6084
M

Coldwell Banker
Pocahontas Realty, Inc.
Route 2, Box 63
Buckeye, WV, USA
(304) 799-6800
M

Coldwell Banker
Armstrong Davis Realty
56 S. Kanawha Street
Buckhannon, WV, USA
(304) 472-7100
M

Coldwell Banker
Taygold Associates, Inc.
1538 Kanawha Blvd. East
Charleston, WV, USA
(304) 346-7774
M

Coldwell Banker
Gerald Warren and Associates
513 Fairmont Avenue
Fairmont, WV, USA
(304) 367-1078
ML

Coldwell Banker
Pancake Realty Company
915 Fifth Avenue
Huntington, WV, USA
(304) 522-8361
M

Coldwell Banker
Terry Stephens & Associates
21 N. Davis Street
Keyser, WV, USA
(304) 788-3322
M

Coldwell Banker
Stuart And Watts Real Estate
114 W. Washington Street
Lewisburg, WV, USA
(304) 645-1242
M

Coldwell Banker
Landmark, Realtors
3201 Murdoch Avenue
Parkersburg, WV, USA
(304) 422-5488
M

Market Type Designations: **M**=Mountain; **D**=Desert;
L=Lake & Stream; **O**=Ocean & Shoreline

WYOMING

Coldwell Banker
The Smith Brokerage
75 N. Main
Buffalo, WY, USA
(307) 684-5563
M

Coldwell Banker
Luker Realty Co.
4221 East 2nd.
Casper, WY, USA
(307) 265-8000
M

Coldwell Banker
Antlers Realty, Inc.
Box 1452, 802 Canyon Avenue
Cody, WY, USA
(307) 587-5533
M

Coldwell Banker
At Whiskey Mountain Realty
Box 1553, 300 W. Ramshorn
Dubois, WY, USA
(307) 455-3722
M

Coldwell Banker
Preferred Realty, Inc.
170 Yellow Creek Rd., Suite A
Evanston, WY, USA
(307) 789-0760
M

Coldwell Banker
Executive Realty
2610 So. Douglas Highway #160
Gillette, WY, USA
(307) 686-7575
M

Coldwell Banker
The Real Estate Co.
Box 1969, 610 W. Broadway
Jackson, WY, USA
(307) 733-7970
M

Coldwell Banker
ABC Realty Company
Box 5056, 856 Coffeen Ave.
Sheridan, WY, USA
(307) 674-7458
M

PUERTO RICO

Coldwell Banker
Isla Del Coqui
Calle 2 A-3 Ext. Villa Rica
Bayamon, PR, Puerto Rico
(787) 787-2920
O

Coldwell Banker
Isla Del Coqui
Avenue Roberto Clemente #115-4
Carolina, PR, Puerto Rico
(787) 757-0707
O

Coldwell Banker
Isla Del Coqui
B-1 Camino Alejandrino
Guaynabo, PR, Puerto Rico
(787) 720-3339
O

Coldwell Banker
Diane Marsters, Inc.
P.O. Box 8755
Humacao, PR, Puerto Rico
(787) 850-3030
O

Coldwell Banker
Tropical Brokers
Ave. Fagot N-19
Ponce, PR, Puerto Rico
(787) 840-0099
O

Coldwell Banker
Isla Del Coqui
651 Avenue San Patricio
Rio Piedras, PR, Puerto Rico
(787) 792-1137
O

Market Type Designations: **M**=Mountain; **D**=Desert;
L=Lake & Stream; **O**=Ocean & Shoreline

Coldwell Banker
Isla Del Coqui
Road 176 KM 01 Cupey
Rio Piedras, PR, Puerto Rico
(787) 765-1652
O

ALBERTA

Coldwell Banker
Kalwest Realty
#202 - 5403 Crowchild Trail N.
Calgary, AB, Canada
(800) 732-9111
M

Coldwell Banker
Rundle Realty
1B - 1000 7th Avenue
Canmore, AB, Canada
(403) 678-3492
M

Coldwell Banker
Best Realty
4905 50th Ave P.O. Box 1499
Cold Lake, AB, Canada
(403) 594-2378
L

Coldwell Banker
Johnston Real Estate
6104 172 Street #223
Edmonton, AB, Canada
(888) 336-7356
L

Coldwell Banker
Haida Realty
5919 - 50th Street
Leduc, AB, Canada
(403) 986-4711
L

Coldwell Banker
City Side Realty
5021-50th Street
Lloydminster, AB, Canada
(403) 875-3343
L

Coldwell Banker
Pristine Southwest Properties
1211 Crocus St., Box 2594
Pincher Creek, AB, Canada
(403) 627-3388
M

Coldwell Banker
Hancock Land Real Estate
52 Broadway N.
Raymond, AB, Canada
(403) 752-3449
L

Coldwell Banker
ONTRACK Realty
7710 50th Avenue
Red Deer, AB, Canada
(403) 343-3344
L

BRITISH COLUMBIA

Coldwell Banker
Lone Butte Realty
715 Alder Ave, Box 2349
100 Mile House, BC, Canada
(250) 395-8500
L

Coldwell Banker
Cranbrook Agencies
1007 Baker Street
Cranbrook, BC, Canada
(250) 426-3355
M

Coldwell Banker
Powder Country Realty
571 2nd Ave. PO Box 1028
Fernie, BC, Canada
(250) 423-6848
M

Coldwell Banker
Horizon Realty
14-1470 Harvey Ave.
Kelowna, BC, Canada
(250) 868-2223
L

Market Type Designations: M=Mountain; D=Desert;
L=Lake & Stream; O=Ocean & Shoreline

Coldwell Banker
Rosling Real Estate
593 Baker St.
Nelson, BC, Canada
(250) 352-3581
M

Coldwell Banker
Desert Aire Realty
34848 - 97th Street Box 1590
Oliver, BC, Canada
(250) 498-4955
D

Coldwell Banker
Okanagan Realty
101-1873 Main Street
Penticton, BC, Canada
(250) 492-2911
DL

Coldwell Banker
Coast Mountain Realty
1705 Campbell Way, Box 550
Port McNeil, BC, Canada
(250) 956-4456
LO

Coldwell Banker
Seacrest Realty
4545 Marine Avenue
Powell River, BC, Canada
(604) 485-2741
LO

Coldwell Banker
First Shawnigan Mill Bay Realty
1750 Shawnigan Mill Bay
Shawnigan Lake, BC, Canada
(250) 743-7151
L

Coldwell Banker
Giants Head Realty
#1 - 10105 Main Street, Box 17
Summerland, BC, Canada
(250) 494-7321
DL

Coldwell Banker
Spectrum Realty
5300 26th Street
Vernon, BC, Canada
(250) 558-4800
L

Coldwell Banker
Sandcastle Victoria Realty
4520 West Saanich Road
Victoria, BC, Canada
(250) 744-1300
O

NEW BRUNSWICK

Coldwell Banker
Keystone Realty
270 Douglas Avenue 4th Floor
Bathurst, NB, Canada
(506) 548-8866
LO

Coldwell Banker
Coughlan Realty
55 Thorne Ave.
Saint John, NB, Canada
(506) 633-0008
O

NOVA SCOTIA

Coldwell Banker
C.R. Cooks Real Estate
215 Dominion Street
Bridgewater, NS, Canada
(902) 543-1888
O

Coldwell Banker
M.B. Green Realty
34 Abercrombie Road
New Glasgow, NS, Canada
(902) 752-1999
L

Coldwell Banker
Tri Key Realty
215 Water St.
Shelburne, NS, Canada
(902) 875-3131
O

Market Type Designations: M=Mountain; D=Desert;
L=Lake & Stream; O=Ocean & Shoreline

Coldwell Banker
Tinkham Real Estate
38 John Street
Yarmouth, NS, Canada
(902) 742-5500
O

ONTARIO

Coldwell Banker
Heritage Way Realty
85 Mill Street, Box 119
Almonte, ON, Canada
(613) 256-5677
L

Coldwell Banker
Valley Wide Real Estate
194 Daniel Street South
Arnprior, ON, Canada
(613) 623-7303
L

Coldwell Banker
Georgian Realty
49 Essa Rd., P.O. Box 1122
Barrie, ON, Canada
(800) 207-5886
LO

Coldwell Banker
Nelles Real Estate
170 North Front Street
Belleville, ON, Canada
(613) 966-1621
L

Coldwell Banker
D. A. Cummings Real Estate
35 Perth Street, P.O. Box 1296
Brockville, ON, Canada
(613) 345-1788
LO

Coldwell Banker
Heritage Way Realty
57 Bridge Street
Carleton Place, ON, Canada
(613) 253-3175
L

Coldwell Banker
Timothy Post Real Estate
6 Church St. W. Box 59
Colborne, ON, Canada
(905) 355-2437
LO

Coldwell Banker
S. Shannon Realty
308 Hurontario Street
Collingwood, ON, Canada
(705) 445-7833
L

Coldwell Banker
Big Creek Realty
R. R. #3
Delhi, ON, Canada
(519) 582-1023
L

Coldwell Banker
Sturino Realty
3825 Bloor St. W.
Etobicoke, ON, Canada
(416) 233-6276
LO

Coldwell Banker
Colonial Realty
200 Garrison Rd., P.O. Box 130
Fort Erie, ON, Canada
(905) 871-7100
LO

Coldwell Banker
All-Points Realty Services
234 Bayfield Road
Goderich, ON, Canada
(519) 524-1175
LO

Coldwell Banker
Thompson Real Estate
70 King William Street
Huntsville, ON, Canada
(705) 789-4957
LO

Market Type Designations: M=Mountain; D=Desert;
L=Lake & Stream; O=Ocean & Shoreline

Coldwell Banker
Graham Thomson Real Estate
166 Wellington Street Box 1056
Kingston, ON, Canada
(613)546-3171
LO

Coldwell Banker
Stonehaven Realty
521 Nottinghill Road, #1
London, ON, Canada
(519) 471-9771
L

Coldwell Banker
Bayline Real Estate
Foot's Bay Muskoka, PO Box 6,
Muskoka, ON, Canada
(705) 375-2333
LO

Coldwell Banker
Peter Minogue Real Estate
382 Fraser Street
North Bay, ON, Canada
(705) 474-3500
LO

Coldwell Banker
First Ottawa Realty
1407 Carling Ave.
Ottawa, ON, Canada
(613) 728-2664
L

Coldwell Banker
Lifestyles Realty
259 10th Street East
Owen Sound, ON, Canada
(519) 372-0990
LO

Coldwell Banker
S.W.E. Heritage Real Estate
70 Joseph
Parry Sound, ON, Canada
(705) 746-7700
LO

Coldwell Banker
Settlement Realty
2 Wilson Street East
Perth, ON, Canada
(613) 264-0123
L

Coldwell Banker
1st Toronto East Realty
1450 Unit 1 Kingston Road
Pickering, ON, Canada
(905) 420-4200
LO

Coldwell Banker
Ostryhon & Balogh Realty
148 Clarence Street
Port Colborne, ON, Canada
(905) 835-2700
L

Coldwell Banker
R.M.R. Real Estate
32 John Street
Port Hope, ON, Canada
(905) 885-1085
LO

Coldwell Banker
F.S.P.Country Lane Realty
5 High St.
Port Perry, ON, Canada
(905) 985-7351
LO

Coldwell Banker
1st Sarnia Real Estate Services
546 N. Christina St.
Sarnia, ON, Canada
(519) 336-7560
O

Coldwell Banker
R. E. Mann Brokers
49 Norfolk Street North
Simcoe, ON, Canada
(800) 567-7423
LO

Coldwell Banker
Sheridan Realty
525 Talbot Street
St. Thomas, ON, Canada
(519) 633-5570
L

Coldwell Banker
Charles Marsh Real Estate (1958)
1090 La Salle Blvd.
Sudbury, ON, Canada
(705) 566-6111
L

Coldwell Banker
Pine Lakes Realty
P. O. Box 449
Sundridge, ON, Canada
(705) 384-5437
L

Coldwell Banker
D.J. Campbell Real Estate
1249 Mosley Street
Wasaga Beach, ON, Canada
(705) 429-4800
LO

PRINCE EDWARD ISLAND

Coldwell Banker
Mol Real Estate
119 University Avenue
Charlottetown, PE, Canada
(902) 892-3404
O

YUKON TERRITORY

Coldwell Banker
Redwood Realty
4150 - 4th Avenue
Whitehorse, YT, Canada
(403) 668-3500
L

Coldwell Banker
Northern Bestsellers
4917-48th Street, PO Box 2138
Yellowknife, YT, Canada
(867) 920-2128
L

Dial 1-888-574-SOLD to locate a Coldwell Banker office in traditional metropolitan markets and other markets not identified in this chapter.

Market Type Designations: M=Mountain; D=Desert;
L=Lake & Stream; O=Ocean & Shoreline

Directory of Other Resources

American Resort Development
Association (ARDA)
1220 L Street, NW
Washington, DC 20005-4059
Phone: (202) 371-6700
Fax: (202) 289-8544

Cendant Mortgage
1-888-CBHOME4

COLDWELL BANKER
Real Estate Corporation
6 Sylvan Way
Parsippany, NJ 07054
Web site: www.coldwellbanker.com

Florida Vacation Rental Managers
Association (FVRMA)
P.O. Box 720684
Orlando, FL 32872-0684
Phone: (407) 658-9504
Fax: (407) 658-6530

International Home Exchange
P.O. Box 190070
San Francisco, CA 94119

Jackson Hewitt Tax Service
4575 Bonney Road
Virginia Beach, VA 23462-3831
Phone: (800) 234-1040
Web site: http://www.jtax.com

Resort Condominiums
International (RCI)
World Headquarters
3502 Woodview Trace
Indianapolis, IN 46268-1104
Phone: (317) 876-1692
Web site: http://www.rci.com

Seltar Interiors
209 South Central Avenue
Oviedo, FL 32765
Phone: (407) 365-5292

Vacation Exchange Club
P.O. Box 820
Haleiwa, HI 96712

Vacation Link
P.O. Box 76350
Atlanta, GA 30358
Phone: (800) 750-0797

Vacation Rental Managers
Association (VRMA)
P.O. Box 1202
Santa Cruz, CA 95061-1202
Phone: (800) 871-8762
Web site: http://www.vrma.com

Index

MONEY SAVING RESORT PROPERTY COUPONS